PAM HLADY's
THE MISHAPS OF TRAVELING

THE MISHAPS OF TRAVELING

PAM HLADY

ISBN: 978-1-967375-20-2 (Paperback)
ISBN: 978-1-967375-21-9 (E-book)

Library of Congress Control Number: 2025911676

Printed in the United States of America

Published by:

info@thequippyquill.com
(302) 295-2278

OUR THEME SONG

Sung by Dean Martin in the '50s

SIDE BY SIDE

[Verse 1]

Oh, we ain't got a barrel of money

Maybe we're ragged and funny

But we'll travel along singing a song

Side by side

We don't know what's coming tomorrow

Maybe it's trouble and sorrow

But we'll travel the road sharing our load

Side by side

[Bridge]

Through all kinds of weather

What if the sky should fall

As long as we're together

It doesn't matter at all

[Verse 2]

When they've all had their quarrels and parted

We'll be the same as we started

Just to travel along singing a song

Side by side

TABLE OF CONTENTS

ON THE RAGGED EDGE

"Pour on the power", I shouted to my husband from the front of the kayak. How could this have happened? We had been the first to leave and now all the other kayaks had passed us up! Yes, we had a head wind, but so did they and they seemed to be rowing smoothly through the Wialua River with great ease, chatting between kayaks as we made our way back to our landing spot.

Well, let me start at the beginning. It was our fortieth wedding anniversary and we had decided to go somewhere we had never been before: Kauai. The Garden Isle. The uppermost island in the chain of Hawaiian islands. We were to be gone for ten days.

I have to admit, as I read about it, it had me worried. It sounded kind of remote and rugged. And the weather this time of year sounded a bit on the cool side: seventy-eight degrees during the daytime. What had we gotten ourselves into?

But not to be daunted by my fears, my husband plowed on ahead and hired AAA to plan our once-in-a-lifetime trip for us. "Spare no expense", he said, "We're going to do this up right." We even decided to fly first class–especially for the long journey over the ocean on the way back where we would have plenty of leg room, pillows and blankets and all the snacks and beverages we could ever want.

Since we were fans of the 1970s TV show, *Hart To Hart*, we sort of fancied ourselves as millionaires, Jonathan and Jennifer Hart. That is partly what helped us decide to fly first class.

On the evening of our trip, my husband presented me with a set of matching monogrammed robes (similar to what

1

Jonathan and Jennifer wore on their show). Oh, my goodness, when I opened his gift, I gasped in surprise, both at the magnitude of his extravagance and at the weight of these robes. They must have weighed about forty pounds apiece! I quickly realized that we would have to put in one per suitcase or there wouldn't be any room for any of our other clothes. I hoped there wasn't a weight limitation on our suitcases.

The day of our trip finally arrived. Beside ourselves with excitement, we practically slept the night before on top of the covers in our traveling clothes. We said a sad goodbye to our dog, Joyful and the lady who was going to be staying with her, and headed out to the airport.

Our adventure began, it seems, as we were going through the line in the airport to get to our plane. Having several carry-ons in our hands plus our passports, photo IDs, reading material and tickets, it was a challenge to get on the other side of the metal detector. It never fails--my husband sets off the metal detector every time and just about ends up in his skivvies by the time I see him on the other end. This time was no different except that after showing the security guard his ID, he apparently upended his wallet and all his credit cards fell out. This put a definite halt to that line while he and the security guard scrabbled around on the floor trying to get everything he dropped. When we finally got seated, he leaned over to me and said, "I feel like I'm living my life on the ragged edge here."

The flight across the Pacific Ocean went without a hitch. We luxuriated in our first-class seats, enjoying all the extra bennies, giving no thought to those poor slobs back in coach, as we once had been.

Landing in Oahu, I took out our GPS that I had brought from home to get us around the streets in Oahu and Kauai. But to my chagrin, my GPS didn't have Hawaii programmed into it. So right off the bat, we were horribly lost trying to find our hotel. After three stops for directions, including one from a policeman, we arrived at our hotel.

And of course, the first thing my husband insisted on doing upon our arrival was to don our new forty-pound bathrobes and go down for a swim in the pool! Now, you have to understand that the Hawaiians, perhaps because they're out in the middle of the ocean, save on things we Mainlanders don't bother about. And at this hotel, while you could get air conditioning in your rooms, it wasn't air conditioned in the hallways and elevators. So wearing a forty-pound bathrobe in an eighty-degree hallway was ludicrous. We definitely got stares from other folks on the elevator. One lady even asked us if we were going down to the hot tub, probably believing we anticipated a cold trip back to our room.

They also seemed to have some new systems in Hawaii that I did not remember from our 1980's Maui trip. In one hotel, we had to use our key card in the elevator to get above the tenth floor. It made no sense to me that terrorists or burglars, if they were going to hit the hotels, would wait until the tenth floor to burgle the rooms. In another hotel, we had to memorize a six-digit code to get into our rooms. And in a third hotel, we had to swipe a card key on the outside of the elevator, punch in the floor number, and quickly jump into it to take us to our floor.

Parking was interesting too. *EVERY* hotel had only valet parking. They charged $25 a day for parking and you were expected to tip the valets every time they brought the car down. Now, maybe Jonathan and Jennifer Hart would have taken that in their stride, but we were cheap and decided to walk most places just to avoid the tips.

Having been the last of the holdouts on landlines, a few months before the trip, we finally broke down and purchased cell phones, despite having tried them unsuccessfully years ago. But we thought we would use them as our cameras on this vacation as well. I told my husband to be sure and bring his too or it was going to look like he was the only one present on our fortieth wedding anniversary because I would be taking all the pictures. Well, lo and behold, Tom did exactly what I told him not to do: he forgot his cell phone. Therefore, most of our pictures on the trip were of him. But as it turned out, at the end of the trip, I had to have my phone rebooted and we lost all of our pictures in the factory reset anyway.

Because Hurricane Ana was out in the Pacific Ocean heading towards Hawaii, it rained the entire time we were on Oahu. But we decided not to let it dampen our spirits.

Our first leg of the adventure was to find our way to the Hard Rock Café where we would get a "free" American breakfast and meet up with Pleasant Holidays who would be helping us plan whatever tours we desired while on our trip. We decided to walk to avoid tipping the valet. And on the way, I suggested we stop off in a small gift shop because I had lost my lipstick on the plane and didn't have another one. And believe me, I am one of these people who, as my husband says, looks lipless without lipstick. When we got in the store, I realized they catered to the Polynesian complexion because the only type of lipstick offered was pink shades, and I am definitely the orange fall type. But the sales clerk assured me that it was "magic" lipstick, that once I put it on, it would magically change into my color.

What can I say? There's a sucker born every second! I put it on and kept checking with my husband to see if it was changing colors yet. But alas, it stayed pink. At least my lips had color.

So off we went to our free breakfast. We made our choices for things we wanted to do while on Kauai and got off, I thought, quite inexpensively. We only spent $600 on excursions. We chose a chocolate farm tour, a tour of a mansion on the southern shore and a kayak/hike trip to see the Secret Falls, so named because the royalty that ruled the islands once lived in that area and it was their secret falls where they swam and dallied. We also rented bicycles for the week at our hotel so we could scour the back streets of Kauai. This proved to be a joke because we were so busy with excursions, we never had time to bike anywhere!

We had three ways we could get to the Secret Falls: we could ride up in a mini bus and ride down again, we could ride in a mini bus and bike down or we could kayak up the river and hike to the falls. Tom chose the bike down the mountain and I chose the kayak/hike. The brochure said it was an "easy paddle in by kayak and then a short hike up to the falls". Naturally, Tom, ever the peacemaker, agreed to my plan.

After leaving Pleasant Holidays, we were offered another "free" gift at a jewelry store. We went by excursion bus to somewhere in the middle of Honolulu to the Hawaiian Pearl Divers. Upon our arrival, they whisked us up to the third floor where they demonstrated how the pearl divers discovered these gems in the Islands. Of course, this being a Saturday, no one was working there, but they showed us each of the stations in the process of choosing the best pearls, polishing them and getting them ready for sale in the jewelry store.

Then we were ushered to the sales floor. The prices were definitely out of our price range, even if we did fancy ourselves to be like Jonathan and Jennifer Hart. We moved from one jewelry case to another, a sales clerk always nearby to engage us in whatever piece we were admiring at the moment.

Finally, we reached the exit. But wait, they weren't done with us. I got to the elevator by which we had come up, and they told us we could take the stairs down to the main floor.

What they didn't tell us is that there was no way out from that room.

But like lambs led to the slaughter, we took the stairs down to level three and was greeted by a small older Asian woman who told us she would sell us whatever pearl we would find inside of an oyster shell for only $14.95. All we had to do is tap it three times and say "Aloha". And what to my wondering eyes should appear, but two pink pearls. "Ah", my Chinese sales lady exclaimed," two for the price of one."

As I was about to take my pearls and go, she ushered us over to another station where we "must" pick out a setting for these pearls. Would I prefer a necklace or a ring? The prices made me gasp. Then when she learned it was our fortieth wedding anniversary (never give sales people any information because they will glom onto it and use it to get you to buy the store!), she knew we just *had* to have this necklace in remembrance of our special time.

Not only was the setting for the pearls expensive, but even the chain was another cost! I tried to tell her that I could just take the setting home and go to Harry's Jewelry and pick up a chain, but she insisted I should have a special chain for this unique gift.

Now, where was my husband, you might ask. Well, maybe he was in shock--I don't know, but he wasn't answering, and I felt like I was swimming upstream fighting off the sharks all by myself.

Every argument I could raise, the sales lady had an answer for. She said we could purchase this beautiful necklace on credit and pay it off within six months with no interest incurred. So finally, we said yes. Then while we waited for her to draw up the papers, we wandered around the shop. And always, no matter what we looked at, we would suddenly find a saleswoman at our elbow extoling us with the virtues of whatever it is we were looking at. By the time we left, we owed them $600!

The following day we headed out to the airport to fly to Kauai and were told that our Island Air flight had been cancelled. Now, you have to understand about the Polynesian culture. Their faces are expressionless when they tell you their news and you walk away in a hopeless state because Hawaii feels like you're in a foreign land.

As we sat and deliberated on our predicament and called AAA to see if they could do anything, the manager came out of his office and told us he could get us on another flight to Kauai that would leave an hour from now. We thanked him profusely and walked, rolling our suitcases behind us, to the plane we were to catch.

On our first day in Kauai, we were scheduled to take our kayak/hike trip to the Secret Falls. Why is it that we always downplay the *news* when we hear it, thinking "Oh, that's no big deal, we can handle that"? Our guide warned us that due to the recent rains, the hike up to the Secret Falls was quite muddy. But I assured him that we could handle it.

Thus, we joined the small group also making the trip and headed out in the van to take us to the river. They helped us into our two-man kayaks and gave us brief instructions on how to paddle them. Actually, the first leg of the trip went quite well. Tom and I quickly fell into a good rhythm and glided swiftly down the stream. Andy, our guide was fascinating as he told us about the flora and fauna we passed, about the 24-hour hibiscus, which started out yellow in the morning and turned bright red toward the end of the day, the history of the island and the stories of the royal families that ruled the islands.

Finally, we landed where the hike would begin. Yes, it did seem a bit muddy where we tied up our kayaks, but I was sure it would be just fine. We all took walking sticks, although I wasn't sure what we would need them for. But I was soon to find out.

Apparently, old irrigation ditches for the royal family's water supply served as our path. So our hike consisted of scaling really large rocks. And the further we got into the path, the slipperier they became. In some places, our feet sank into muddy water up to our ankles. I was the only one who fell not once, but twice on our trek up the path. Though Tom teetered and tottered, he was able to at least keep his balance. The man at the end of our troupe finally gave me his walking stick so that I had two in order to keep my balance. And the guide, on our way back, kept walking beside me with his hands out ready to catch me should I fall again. I'm sure he had some interesting tales to tell his family that night at supper about the old lady who kept falling on the hike up the path!

Once we reached the falls, it was almost anticlimactic. Though it was magnificent, having forded the river three times with the help of a tow rope and slipped and slid along the path, I felt like I had reached the top of Mount Everest.

While our group frolicked in the cool water beneath the waterfalls in our muddy clothes, we were too tired to care when we finally got there. Meanwhile, Andy laid out a lunch for us on a huge boulder complete with orchid petals and pineapple slices.

I had the feeling that maybe Andy was sort of happy to get rid of Tom and I, because when we reached the spot where our kayaks were parked, he said, "You two go on ahead, we'll catch up with you." We left that place in a hurry and I was sure we'd be sitting on the shore waiting for the group to "catch up". But like I said in the beginning, though we were going as fast as we could, the group caught up and passed us by. But seeing our landing gave me renewed hope.

When we got back to our condo, I decided to try to dry our leather sneakers in the dryer. Each room had its own washer and dryer. Then I proceeded to try to wash out our sneakers in the kitchen sink, rinsing them several times before I threw them in the dryer. But I guess I didn't get them clean enough because when the dryer went off, Tom opened it to discover that the entire dryer was coated with river sand, and because it was hot in the dryer, the sand had actually baked onto the walls.

Tom took one look and shook his head and just closed the door. Nor did he tell me he had looked in the dryer. Later while he was out doing something, I looked in the dryer and couldn't believe my eyes. My only thought was that I had to get this cleaned out before Tom saw it. So painstakingly, I repeatedly wiped down each portion of the walls with a wet white bathmat (what other color do you find in hotels and resorts?), wringing it out in the kitchen sink between wipes. By the time I got done, an hour later, the dryer was white again, but the bathmat looked like I had cleaned the bottom of my car with it. But then, I had to repeatedly rinse it to get the towel clean - all while Tom was out so that he wouldn't get mad at me for what I had done. The next day we discovered that our shoes had shrunken, probably due to both the water and the dryer heat. So we had to go out and purchase new shoes.

The island of Kauai was beautiful though. It truly is a garden isle. We traveled by car as far north as we could go and as far south as we could go. On the furthest north point we went swimming on Ke'e Beach. They had interesting lifeguard stations. They looked like a camper someone put up on stilts. The beaches were mildly busy, but parking was definitely a commodity.

One other excursion we made while there was a trip on a large boat up the same river we had kayaked, to see the Fern

Grotto. Our traveling companions was a large group of senior citizens who had come from a cruise ship. Though I could be considered in the beginning stages of that demography, I had thus far refused to join them because I've never wanted to be thought of as in a certain group.

Due to the boat's passengers with few people of other ages, the band clearly catered to them. They invited all the seniors to stand and learn how to hula. Somehow, I felt like I had stepped into a room full of toddlers as I watched them swaying to the music and mimicking the hand motions.

When we arrived at the Fern Grotto fifteen minutes later (this was a short ride compared to our kayak trip), we had a brief walk on a paved path (a far cry from the hike I had taken a couple days ago on a muddy path) to the grotto which was basically a large cave with greenery hanging down in front of it. Since it was known as a wedding venue, Tom and I decided to sort of renew our wedding vows while they sang and played the Hawaiian Wedding Song for the senior citizens. Then we all trooped back to the boat and rode back to the landing.

On the final day of our vacation, we decided to take a helicopter ride to see the Nai Pali coast, which can only be seen by boat or helicopter, since there is a road on that part of the island. Now, THAT was a highlight. I was a little nervous because I'd never flown in a helicopter before, but it was as smooth as flying on the wings of a bird. From the air we saw a myriad of waterfalls, including the one used in the Jurassic Park movie, we flew down into a crater and swung out over the Nai Pali coast.

To travel back to Oahu, our flight didn't leave until that evening. And when we got to the airport, first, our plane was going to be delayed and then finally, they cancelled it altogether. So that meant that the harried desk clerks had to reroute each of us on different flights or give us a hotel to stay in overnight. Never mind the fact that only two clerks were waiting on over two hundred people.

When we finally got to the counter, they told us we could fly out tonight, but they couldn't guarantee us first-class on the first leg of our trip. But we decided to chance it.

What a mistake! They put us on an Airbus in the center of the plane with virtually no leg room, and it was very cold. We felt like sardines packed for shipping. It reminded me of a Greyhound bus trip we took a couple of years ago to get to Minneapolis for the State Fair. It was a terrible ride and exactly why we booked first class in the first place – so we could ride the seven-hour trip over the ocean in comfort.

And when we arrived stateside, while waiting for the next plane, we were treated like coach fares and barred from being able to wait in the captain's lounge without paying a fee. We decided to bite the bullet and pay the fee so we could pretend we were Jonathan and Jennifer a little longer.

But as in all things make make-believe, we had to leave the Harts behind and return to our normal lives. We have no pictures to prove we were in Kauai for two weeks, but oh, the memories we carry inside our hearts!

THE DREAM THAT TURNED INTO A NIGHTMARE

"It will be the dream ski vacation of our lives", my husband assured me. "Remember Canada?" We had been on a winter ski trip to Canada two years earlier and I had to admit that it turned out to be a great trip. But I had serious misgivings about this one.

It was a backcountry cross-country ski trip in Colorado. I thought being stateside, it might be safer. During World War II the troops had trained in these huts in the Rockies and it was now a hiker's and skier's paradise called Hut-To-Hut. I was about to learn to trust my gut instinct!

Tom had gotten the idea from some co-workers who worked in the insurance industry in Colorado. He came home, glowing with what an adventurous time we'd have. Then he called Hut-To-Hut and had a brochure mailed to us. He also ordered a book that described in living detail the splendor of a Hut-to-Hut trip. For him this was *"Cabin Island"* with the Hardy Boys all over again. Only this time *I* got to go along too.

Receiving the brochure, he read it aloud to me. The brochure warned us that this trip was not for the novice skier. "But we're intermediate skiers", Tom assured me, "we can handle this".

As the time got closer to the upcoming trip, I became more and more anxious. Tom, catching some of my anxiety, called the lady organizing the trip and shared our concerns with her. "Nonsense", she cried, "Why, this is the easiest package you can purchase. You only stay in one cabin, instead of skiing hut to hut like the experts did, and you just ski right out your back door". Thus, once again, my husband allayed my fears.

In Denver we had planned to get acclimated to the high altitude by staying an extra day before we set off, but we had car trouble on the way down and didn't have time to do that. At Recreational Equipment, Inc. (REI), a local ski rental place, they "outfitted" us with all the gear we would need for our trip: cross-country skis, snake skins to snap on and off for climbing hills, special boots, poles, sleeping bags, our dehydrated food, dishes and of course a backpack. Spending much time instructing us in the fine art of putting on a backpack, we hoped we were finally ready.

We did practice packing and putting on the backpack in the hotel room that night. I was amazed at how heavy that thing was. We hadn't even ever done any hiking before. And here we were hiking with backpacks on and skiing all at the same time! But of course, in the hotel room, it still didn't seem real.

The next day we drove up to the place where the trail began. Our car would, of course, stay parked there until we came back three days later. We were surprised to see how many other cars there were there. But the trails accommodated both snowmobilers and cross-country skiers.

The brochure had encouraged us to bring a water bottle because due to the altitude, one can become dehydrated very easily. We brought a quart thermos each that I had purchased at Starbuck's more because I thought it was "cute", but we thought we wouldn't bring it out until we got into camp. After all, it probably wouldn't take us that long to ski to the cabin.

On the way in to the trail, we met the skiers who were coming back from the cabin we were heading to. To my chagrin, I noticed that there weren't any women amongst the group and it occurred to me that maybe this was a man's sport more than a woman's. But you-know-who convinced me that that wasn't the case.

The other group assured us it was an easy hour-and-a-half ski to the lodge. "Oh", they added, "by the way, the gas burning stove downstairs doesn't work properly, so it will get down to about forty degrees at night." It didn't sound too promising. But I decided that I would keep a positive attitude.

We started out on the ski trail and found it very slow going. I had donned my "skins", as the snake skins are called, so that going up the steeper hills wouldn't be so difficult. The clerk at REI had assured me that they snap right on and then you can snap them right off when you need to glide down the hill. Well, that was an understatement! They snapped on with the aid of four buckles around the skis and attached at both the tip and rear of the ski. When I had them on, they had no glide whatsoever and it felt like I was snowshoeing instead of skiing. As for snapping them off easily at the top of a hill, it was a joke! They snapped off about as easily as they snapped on!

Another problem I had was with the skis. One of them kept disengaging from my foot every time it got snow in between the toe and the latch on the ski! So I was constantly having to stop and wipe off my foot and then get it anchored back in the ski. (We later found out that there was something mechanically wrong with the ski).

But the major problem we were both having was the altitude and the fact that we had no water with us. We assumed that we would feel thirsty if we got dehydrated. But instead, what we would feel is lightheaded and dizzy! Every fifty feet we stopped and rested. One of our cabin mates, Ted, a man from St. Paul, Minnesota, glided up behind us about halfway through the trip and kept giving us drinks from his water bottle. He probably thought where did these two loony-tooners come from!

The weather in the mountains can change in an instant. One minute the sun can be out and the next, you can be in the middle of a blizzard. Such was our trek across the Rockies.

By the time we arrived at our cabin, it was about three hours later and I was extremely cold. While Tom and Ted fought with the lock to the lower cabin, I went upstairs. I must have looked like Nanooka From The North to the four guys in the upper unit. They pushed me down in a blue, plastic chair and shoved this hot bean soup in my hand. And, can you believe this, I was so cold that I actually ate it (and I hate bean soup). They had a blazing fire in a wood burning stove and it took about twenty minutes for me to finally thaw out. This unit was so warm that one of the guys was actually wandering around in his long underwear and bare feet!

The four guys upstairs, it turned out, were former college roommates who continued to get together for a yearly adventure. This was their adventure for this year. But they proved to be companionable guys. They invited us to bring our dehydrated food upstairs in the evenings to join them for supper. They would only be staying for one more day, and since there were no other people around, we took advantage of their hospitality.

Our own unit slept six. There were two bedrooms, each with two beds and two beds in the living room. It also had a bathroom, kitchen, appliances and a table and chairs. Ted, it turned out, was someone who had done this trip many times before and loved it, kept encouraging us.

The gas heater was a bit cold for us, but I had brought along hot water bottles for inside our sleeping bags, and we just slept with all of our clothes on for warmth. The other times, we hiked upstairs to join the "fellows". Being I was the only woman in the crowd, the guys did have to watch their language, for which I was thankful.

In a situation like that, everyone became everyone else's buddy. We all assured each other that we would keep in touch when we got back to civilization and exchange pictures of our magnificent journey into the wilderness.

The scenery up here *was* gorgeous. The hills were dotted with evergreen trees that went on for miles in every direction. At night, it was so dark I couldn't see my hand in front of my face. On clear nights, we loved looking at the constellations. And like the weather on the way to the cabin, it could change in a moment.

The next day we decided to try the ski trails. We had to be careful, however, because we were warned that we were in avalanche country. Tom and I had recently seen a story of an avalanche on the weather channel, and thus, had a healthy respect for them. So we decided to stay away from those trails up higher in the mountains.

At first Ted was going to ski elsewhere, so we decided to bring walkie-talkies so that if either he or we got into trouble, we could contact one another. This wasn't like your local ski resort, where there are lots of other skiers out on the trails. It was remote in the strictest sense of the word.

But finally, he decided to go with us. We were told that there was a ski trail right outside our cabin that did not lead to avalanche territory. On our way up the hill, we met our upper unit comrades coming down. As I stepped off the trail to let them pass, I discovered why it wasn't a good idea to get off the trails. I found myself in snow up to my waist! Two of the guys reached down and pulled me up by my armpits like a rag doll to get me back on the trail again.

Because the trails were basically snowed over, it was not easy going like groomed trails. I took my skins, but didn't use them very much since I couldn't don and remove them quickly. Coming down hills could be pretty zippy. I was just glad to get back to the cabin for hot soup. Tom and Ted went out after lunch to ski some more, but Tom ended up in some creek bed at the bottom of a hill, and Ted didn't fare much better.

We had our last supper with our friends upstairs the night before they were leaving. It was a sad farewell, they were nice guys. And Ted was also leaving shortly thereafter, so Tom and I decided to move upstairs just for a warmer atmosphere when our friends vacated it.

Knowing Ted was leaving in the morning, I kind of hinted that maybe we would just go with him. It seemed safer to me, but he couldn't understand why we would give up the extra night we had booked to stay in this wonderful place and miss all the fantastic skiing. So we decided that we wouldn't tell him, but we would be going home after he left the next morning. We didn't want to burst his bubble.

That night, for the first time in my life, I had the closest thing to a panic attack. The thought of being alone there, of having to put my backpack on by myself, and of having to find our way back to civilization by ourselves was just more than I could handle. In the middle of the night, my heart began to pound so loudly, it woke me up. I woke Tom up, of course, and he calmed me down so I could sleep. My fear abated, but I was still pretty anxious.

The next morning, I watched out the window as Ted left to go back home, and I felt that familiar longing to be going with him. After our breakfast, however, we made our preparations. We locked up the cabin, knowing that we would never return again.

Surprisingly, we were able to don our backpacks, but they weren't on properly. At one point on the trail, I called to Tom and said "I feel like this thing has a death grip on me".

"That's nothing", he replied, "I feel like it has a death grip on one side, but my bra strap keeps slipping on the other side!"

Further down the trail I fell over and felt like a gigantic turtle flipped over on its back. I had to take the backpack completely off in order to get back on my feet, and then put it back on.

We decided to take the snowmobile trail back since it was marked better than the ski trail. But we were taking our life in our hands traveling it. Though we stayed off to the side, the snowmobiles traveled at such high speeds that they came upon us too fast for them to slow down. But none of them got angry at us because we were on their trails.

Finally, we got back to our car, which was buried with the many snowstorms it had undergone. But we were happy to dig it out and be on our way.

LIFE ON WHEELS

It could have been a scene from "The Long, Long Trailer" with Lucy and Desi Arnaz. For that matter, it could have been the whole movie – well, not quite.

Being inveterate tent campers for twenty-eight years, we finally decided to upgrade to a pop-up camper. As we were getting older, I discovered that it was getting harder for me to get in and out of the tent in a crawl position. So after perusing the *Thrifty Nickel*, we found a 1968 Scamper pop-up camper. To my delight, the price was right and we bought it.

The day that we were to pick it up soon arrived and my husband, Tom and I drove over with great eagerness. The previous owners, Steve and Jamie took us through a hands-on demonstration of how to take it down, and Steve even took my husband out for a drive with it so he could get used to how it felt on the road. And he also helped Tom learn how to back up, cautioning Tom that if he backed up too quickly, the camper could double back and hit the car. But after much maneuvering, Tom finally learned how to back it up.

We drove it home without a hitch – no pun intended. But I must admit that I kept looking back to see if it was still with us – fully expecting it to go one way on the freeway while we went the other way – so great was my faith.

That weekend we had originally planned on going camping and Tom had even taken that Friday off. So what could be more perfect than that we would take the camper out. But Steve and Jamie, we learned, at the end of the transaction, had failed to get the title in their names from the person they bought it from. And though they could get a "quick title", one on short notice, we wouldn't be able to get the title switched to our names until the following Monday.

But not to be too discouraged, we decided to camp out in our driveway that first weekend. It was the hottest weekend on record – ninety degrees all weekend. We did not let the heat get us down. As true, blue troopers, we commenced to set up our camper and determined we would sleep in it and eat in it just like a real camping trip – let the neighbors think what they wanted. But I must admit that I looked for opportunities to have to go in the air-conditioned house for "things" to use in the camper!

Actually, we did put the camper up with very little problem. We only had to make one trip to the hardware store when we broke a roller on the pole that pops the roof up. This only strengthened our thankfulness that we made the right decision in camping at home that weekend.

Finally, we got our hacienda up. And oh, how we marveled at its spaciousness. Soon we were eating our first meal in it by electric light and with running water! We thought we had died and gone to heaven!

That night all of us--including the dog who was settling onto the couch—climbed into bed. I was a bit fearful that the bed might collapse, having heard a story from a friend the previous week about another inexperienced couple who had gone camping and having failed to put the aluminum poles under the beds for support, slept all night with their camper looking like a big-winged marooned bird. And even though I checked and double-checked our aluminum poles, I was still afraid that they would give way in the middle of the night. But we both made it safely and comfortably through the night.

The next morning, I further stretched my wings by cooking on the stove for the first time. I served a scrumptious breakfast of French toast and sausages to my ravenous husband. By that evening, you'd have thought we were pros.

Tom even built a wood fire in the barbeque grill so we could roast marshmallows and have S'mores!

We knew we were now ready for the real thing. And that opportunity came a few weeks later when we decided to camp out at Raccoon Lake Recreational Campground in Rockville, Indiana.

Since Tom could not take that Friday off, we had to leave when he got home from work at six o'clock. We worried that it could be dark by the time we got there, thus, we drove as quickly as we could to the campground.

After paying the park fee, we oohed and ah-ed over the beauty of the campground and the spacious campsites. The lakes were plentiful and big. Tom was especially excited because he thought he wouldn't have to back the trailer in and risk the trailer jackknifing on the car. "Look", he exclaimed, "I think many of the campsites have a pull through!"

After a bit of a wait in the gathering dusk, we were finally through the campground gates and on our way to our assigned campsite. Having sent in a refund, I was sure we would be given one of the better campsites.

I couldn't believe my eyes when I saw our campsite. It was on a hilly, pie-shaped, grassless lot with roads going past it on both sides! It looked like we were camping on a median between two freeways! I could only think that in getting our reservation, the campground attendants must have said," Let's give these folks the most undesirable campsite in the park!" And to Tom's dismay, there was no pull-through, he was going to have to back in and in a very narrow space with the neighbors across the way looking on.

For me, it was Desi Arnaz all over again. And like Lucy, I got out of the car in an attempt to direct Tom into the parking place. Fortunately, he did not jackknife and got the trailer in safely. But there wasn't much more room than for the trailer and the car. On the other side of the trailer before the other road began, there was an enormous embankment.

By this time, it was nearly dark. There was hardly enough light to see each other much less to see things on the camper. As we began taking the trailer off the car and putting it on its wheel, to my dismay I noticed that the neighbors next door - only about thirty feet away-had pulled up lawn chairs to watch us put up our camper. We felt like we were on *Saturday Night Live.*

Our first, and what we feared could be our final feat, was getting the pin in through the wheel pole so that we could disengage the trailer. For some reason, though we were both down on the gravel now, trying to see it with a flashlight, we could not find the hole for the pin. Finally, however, we were successful.

Soon we had the trailer propped up on the stands, the beds folded out, the aluminum poles inserted, the windows opened, and the lights on. We only had two mishaps. One roof pole fell down, but our neighbor supplied a bungee cord to hold it up. We couldn't get the door attached properly, but it looked like we could shut it almost, so we decided to leave it until morning. Being hot and tired, we just didn't have the energy to wrestle with it any longer.

It soon became apparent, though, that we weren't having roasted wienies over the fire like I had planned on the menu. For some reason, Tom couldn't get the wood fire going. So we cooked our meal in the camper and made the best of it. We even did the S'mores over the gas flame.

As we climbed wearily into our beds that night, I was just sure that the camper was going to slide down the hill - I was on the downhill side - and I hoped that the car would stop it from careening into the campers across the road!

In the middle of the night, I awoke, and to my horror, I discovered that the door was wide open! Thankfully, our dog was still on the couch inside, but I wondered how long that door had been open. I knew it probably had something to do with the fact that we hadn't been completely successful with getting it put together right, but I didn't know exactly what the problem was. I was soon to find out.

Getting out of bed and stepping over the table, I reached around and pulled the door shut and latched it. Then I climbed back across the table and sat down on my bed again. At that, the door flew open again. The problem was that because we were on a slant and not level ground, every time I sat on my bed, the camper shifted enough to unlatch the door!

Well, this won't do, I thought to myself, especially since I had seen raccoons wandering through our campsite the last time I had gotten up. So in the middle of the night, I was pawing through our belongings in the camper, searching for a rope or something to secure the door. Finally, I found a white cord which I tied around the door handle and the sink faucet to ensure that the door wouldn't open again. With that, I went back to bed and prayed for the best.

Morning dawned, and with the daylight, we discovered we were under a tree where squirrels were storing up nuts for the winter. I got my first introduction to this while I was making breakfast. All of a sudden there was a loud clunk. I jumped and said "What was that?" I thought we had gotten shot at! Tom, who had already figured it out, said "Oh, don't worry, it's only squirrels in the tree above us, dropping cracked acorns on the metal roof of our camper." And that sound was to stay with us all day long. I could just picture the squirrels in the tree making a great sport out of it, yelling, "Geronimo" and flinging their shells, as hard as they could, toward some invisible bull's eye on the top of our camper.

Also, by the light of day, we discovered that the water hand pump was on our property. That meant campers were constantly traipsing through our lot to fill their water jugs.

Really, though, the weekend went off without many more difficulties. We were able to fix the door so that it shut properly. And except for the fact that the unlevel ground caused the cupboard doors to shut fast when I opened them on one side and to fly open on the other side, we soon grew accustomed to our house on wheels.

But by the time we left on Sunday, we were ready to go home. And we thought, as we do in many of our life's experiences, that at least this weekend would give us something to laugh at.

HELP, I'VE BEEN KEEDNAPPED!

VERY IMPORTANT ARRIVAL INFORMATION: In most Mexican destinations, the business of Hotel Timesharing is very apparent. The Timeshare representatives are located in the airport and are very aggressive as they try to sell their hotel timeshare to arriving travelers. *Now* they tell me!

Upon arriving in Mazatlan where we would be vacationing for a week, we exited our plane, only to be confronted with many of these "aggressive" salespeople. We looked around wildly, wondering what to do next. We saw a Resorts Condominium (RCI) salesman, whose timeshare we were staying at, and thought *surely, this must be a safe person to trust in this foreign country.*

Pedro quickly ushered us over to the counter of the timeshare he was representing, dollar signs glowing in his eyes, all the while assuring us that he had our best interests at heart. At the counter a lady explained to us that for simply "touring" the timeshare at The Hawaiian Sunset Hotel, we could get a coupon book that gave us a free ride from the airport to our hotel, two dinners at the Mexican Fiesta, (the best fiesta in town) and several other great deals. My husband and I looked at each other and thought, *what can we lose? Surely, we can sit through a timeshare presentation – after all, look at all these great deals!* And we were hooked.

"But", the timeshare lady warned us, "the Polynesian Inn you're staying at the first night has their own timeshares that they're trying to sell, so avoid the lady who will try to sell you a timeshare there and wait for us across the street from the hotel. We will pick you up at ten o'clock the following morning."

Wearily, we climbed into our "free" taxi and drove to our hotel where we would spend the first night before we could get into our timeshare the next day. The décor in the hotel was beautiful. The pool was on the ocean side, surrounded by white sand and relaxed vacationers. This promised to be just the vacation we were in need of.

But that very afternoon we met Zelda, the ever-smiling, overzealous, timeshare saleslady from the hotel. She could have been anybody's mother. She was a short, round Mexican lady with beautiful black hair who parked herself right in front of the elevators at the hotel, waiting for unsuspecting weary travelers just ripe for the kill. You met her coming and going. But we were smart, we might have been tired, but we soon learned that instead of taking the elevator up and down, if we took the stairs, we could avoid her.

She was as aggressive as we had been warned. She even left her elevator station and followed folks out onto the front steps! And she had a bewildered look on her face when you turned down her efforts to show you these beautiful timeshares she had for sale.

But as we soon learned, Pedro at the airport and Zelda at the Polynesian Inn were just the beginning. Everywhere we went, we were hounded by timeshare people or people selling other things. Out on the beach our first afternoon there, we met people wanting to sell us silver or hats or someone approached us and asked us if we wanted to get "high"! In the restaurants, the maître 'de as well as the waiters and waitresses would all at first appear to be friendly and really interested in you as a tourist, but all had one agenda in mind: sell this dumb American tourist a timeshare.

When we walked down the streets in town at night, we were constantly accosted by aggressive salesmen. When we stopped to snap pictures of buildings, we met people who would willingly take us on a tour. It got to the point where we dared not make eye contact with anyone for fear of being presented with another sales opportunity.

In one restaurant the waiter actually got mad at us when we resisted his efforts to take his tour to sell his timeshare. Our meal was delicious, but we sort of slinked out of the restaurant after rebuffing him. It was obvious we were not welcome unless we spent our American dollars on his timeshare.

But I am getting ahead of myself. The following morning after getting some much-needed rest and being able to avoid Zelda upon exiting the hotel, we waited across the street for Pedro to come pick us up.

Out on the street, we were like sitting ducks. I can't tell you the number of cars, taxis and people walking on the streets that stopped and offered to take us to a timeshare presentation. They had taxicabs that looked like VW bugs with the tops cut off that were called Palmettos. Numerous Palmettos stopped and offered to take us to our destination – no matter where it might be.

The Mexican sales people were not even true to each other! If one could cut out the business of his fellow countryman, he did so with little conscience. And so it was that when one car stopped with two men and a woman in it and we explained that we were waiting for a man named Pedro to take us to the timeshare, they didn't hesitate to tell us that they would take us to Pedro, that Pedro was out at the timeshare waiting for us. So being the naive tourists we were, we readily hopped in the car, believing we were safe at last.

The first time I suspected anything wrong was that the driver was going the wrong way! The night before, we happened to being walking on the street and saw the place where the timeshare tour was going to be taking place – and it was definitely not *this* way. Also, the longer we were in the car, the more remote the countryside was becoming. When I brought up the fact that they seemed to be going the wrong way, my illustrious tour guides assured me that all the timeshare places were linked and that Pedro was waiting for us.

When we arrived at our destination, I could not believe my eyes. It was a building that was just in the beginning stages of construction, it was all cement. We were led up into the portico or the foyer where I assumed the front desk might reside one day (you could tell that by the cement pillars surrounding the front area) and out back were men hauling cement in wheelbarrows and virtually building the rest of the site by hand!

In the middle of the foyer was an oversized desk that seemed more like somebody's dining room table. And on one side of it was one chair and then on our side were two plush red cushioned chairs that we were invited to sit in. On the desk top was brightly colored literature. But Pedro was nowhere to be seen.

We sat down in the comfortable seats and the new salesman explained to me that this timeshare was in the process of being built and told us what the projected date of its completion would be. Then he showed us from the literature what the building would look like upon its completion.

However, I had my wits about me at least. I asked to see Pedro. Surely Pedro would protect me. There was one cement wall behind the desk a few paces through which my drivers had escaped. At my demand to see Pedro, they re-emerged and informed me that Pedro had gone back out to the airport!

At that proclamation, I started realizing we'd been had. And the salespeople started upping the ante to purchase their timeshare. Pounding my fist on the table, I finally said, "You take me back to my hotel right now or I'm going to start walking!!!" So they put us back in the Palmetto and drove us back to our hotel, all the time promising us more and more if we bought their timeshare.

The next morning, we arrived at our timeshare, thinking once again, we were on safe territory. After all, we had arrived at our destination unscathed, but extremely exhausted both from fighting the timeshare people and just sadly in need of a vacation. And that, my friend, turned out to be a major detriment to us.

After checking in, we were ushered over to a table in the lobby to another lovely Mexican woman who explained in broken English that if we toured the current timeshare we were staying in, we would get lots of coupons for the various things we could see on our stay in Matzalan.

Now, we had been in timeshare for a number of years, but had never traveled in a foreign country. In the stateside timeshares, it was an option to tour the timeshare in which you were staying. It was low key and not mandatory. But we thought maybe in Mexico you *had* to go on the tour. And being really weary, we thought *what the heck, we can sit through "an hour and a half timeshare presentation*, as they had promised us. So we agreed to do it the next day – we wanted to get it out of the way so we could enjoy the rest of our stay. And after all, they promised us breakfast as well. What could go wrong?

The next day arrived and we met a timeshare saleslady at a lovely breakfast onsite and we chatted comfortably with one another. Then she led us into a large room that was obviously doing a BIG business. Throughout the room there were round tables with lovely linen tablecloths on them, salespeople seated usually with a couple of dumb tourists like ourselves.

We listened to the presentation, but we knew we weren't going to buy, so we gently kept telling Carlotta "Thank you, but we just aren't interested." Now, Carlotta might have been new, but she was smooth. She explained that because she was new, would we mind having her boss stop over – just to make sure she had done everything correctly. Thus, we said "Sure, fine, send him over." What a mistake!

Glenn, her boss, was a young man of about 35, married and a brand new father. And he was suave. He knew how to break the Americans and get them to part with their brass.

When we'd say "no", he'd say "yes", when we'd say "no, no, no", he'd say "yes, yes, yes". And like his countrymen before him, he kept upping the ante. I think by the time we signed on the dotted line and left (just because we couldn't hold up on under the torture), he had upped the ante from one week to three weeks, assuring us that we could even rent the units out and make money on them. And the one-and-a-half hour timeshare tour had stretched into six hours!

Carlotta, needless to say, was thrilled to be selling her first timeshare. She even sent us a beautiful bouquet of flowers to let us know how much she enjoyed working with us.

But by the next day, it finally dawned on us what we did. Now, we knew we had three days by contract to break out of the deal. So we went down the next morning to speak to Glenn. But that morning, Glenn was "unavailable", another salesperson said, "come back this afternoon." But that afternoon he was still unavailable nor was he available the next day. As we were getting near the end of our three days, I decided to write him a letter and tell him we wanted out of the contract.

Well, that must have gotten his attention. Finally, he agreed to meet with us in his office that day. Glenn just looked so bewildered as to why we didn't want this beautiful timeshare, and a little hurt, I might add. His wife even stopped by for a visit - with the new little Bambino cradled in her arms. (I couldn't help but wonder if that wasn't

staged for our benefit too!)

Though we were adamant in our decision, Glenn suggested we come back tomorrow and if we still felt the same, he would tear up our contract. Hence, one more day passed, but you would have been proud of us. We stood our ground.

It wasn't until the day before we were due to fly back to the States that our contract became null and void, and our vacation truly began. It was unbelievable how light we felt in our spirits that day. Tom went parasailing and we went on a tour of the city. But on the tour, we heard a similar horror story to ours. Apparently, another couple got locked into a contract just like we did, and they ended up having to call in the American Embassy to get them out of hot water!

THE LONG, LONG BUS RIDE

Well, okay, so I admit that we made our decision to travel from Texas to Minnesota by Greyhound bus based on my childhood memories of three-hour trips between Minneapolis and Mankato to visit my grandmother. Those were wonderful trips. The bus drivers were nice, the passengers were nice – regular people like we were – the small towns we went through were exciting and you could be assured of a stop for lunch in one of the bus stations where you could get a great restaurant cooked meal.

So of course, with those warm fuzzy memories, we decided to take the bus home for a long weekend to attend the Minnesota State Fair – one of the best state fairs in the country, I might add. I thought this would be an ideal way to go. It would be a quick four-day trip. We could travel all night and have a nice sleep on the bus and then wake up in Minneapolis, go to the fair for a day and get back on the bus for a nice trip home. NOT.

Things certainly have changed in the Greyhound bus industry since when I was a child.

The bus drivers were no longer friendly, they seemed more distrusting, the passengers have denigrated to the people who basically have no cars and yet needed to get from one short distance to another, the bus stations were in some of the worst areas of town and instead of nice lunch counters, most were filled with vending machines.

The night before our trip, we slept in our traveling clothes because we had to get up at four a.m. to get to the bus on time. The only problem was that at some point during the night, due to a storm, the power went off and so I kept checking my watch every fifteen minutes so that we wouldn't miss the cab that was taking us to the bus station. We made it okay, but the cabbie, in an effort to protect these two unsuspecting passengers, gave us dire warnings about the muggings and other criminal activities we could experience at the hands of the unsavory people who hung around bus terminals.

Upon boarding the bus, we soon learned that we were on a milk run. We could have taken an express bus, but didn't know about it. The express bus would have only stopped at the major cities, and was more expensive while the one we were on stopped at every little city along the route, including the major cities. And it seemed like every five minutes, they stopped for a potty break.

Inside the bus, it definitely wasn't what I fondly remembered from my youth. There was virtually no leg room, my seat didn't tilt back at all and the seats were as hard as rocks.

The bus driver was up front in some sort of plastic cage that kept him from hearing whatever might have been going on behind him. I wondered if the plastic was bulletproof too!

It was very, very cold in the bus for which we were unprepared. I'm sure you'll laugh at me, but I looked around and noticed some passengers had blankets, so I thought maybe the overhead bins were like those on a plane and they had pillows and blankets in them for the passengers. At one point, I sent Tom up front to the bus driver to ask if we could have a pillow and a blanket. Tom came back up the aisle towards me, shaking his head in the negative. Apparently, you could purchase a small blanket in the bus station, but we didn't know about that either! So we froze to death until we could get to a bus station where we could open our suitcases and look for warmer clothing.

Finally, we purchased a blanket in one of the larger stations, but it must have been a cheap blanket because it left lint all over our clothing every time we covered up in it. And we also rummaged around in our suitcase for Tom to put on something long-sleeved. The only thing we could find was his pajama tops. But by that time, we really didn't care how it looked, only that we could get warm.

The other interesting thing was that the bus driver apparently controlled the lights over the passengers. when it was nighttime, it didn't matter if you went to bed at this time of the night or not, it was lights out! No reading lights except if you brought a flashlight.

So here we thought we had planned well for the trip. We brought a small suitcase with three books a piece and some games, believing that we would be occupied with at least reading during the trip! Our books pretty much remained in the suitcase for the duration of the trip – or at least until daylight. And there were no tray tables on the back of the seats in front of us, since they didn't serve us snacks like the airplanes did – another misnomer of mine. So our games pretty much stayed in the suitcase too and even if we could have played games, the seats in front of us were so close, it was an impossibility.

The bus drivers varied in attitude, love for their job and friendliness to the passengers. I guess to most of them, this was just a job and they basically weren't too fond of it.

The first one was Eddie. He definitely had a problem with road rage. For the least little infraction, he would lay on the horn and shake his fist at the vehicle in front of him. And I'm sure his size as a vehicle truly put the fear of God in a lot of people. He also seemed to be somebody that didn't like traveling on the beaten path (the freeway). He veered off on to back country roads as he traveled from town to town. At least the scenery was interesting.

There was Clem who gave humorous instructions and kept talking about keeping your "stanky" feet out of the aisles when you sit in your seats so that others could get through the aisle to get to the bathroom.

Then there was Brad who was a no-nonsense sort of guy, who refused to pick up a passenger in Austin because he was a few minutes late. He told the sad-faced college student he would have to wait for the next bus that would come in about twelve hours!

Then there was John who was really focused in on his homemade lunch. Though us passengers were met with only vending machines to provide us with lunch, his wife had apparently packed him a great lunch of two sandwiches, carrot sticks, potato chips and dessert. While the rest of us suffered on packaged dry meals, we watched a play-by-play of John slowly going through his lunch. We kept saying to each other, "now he's opening his other sandwich..." John ate so slow, it was apparent that he was hoping his eight-course lunch would last him through his entire journey.

And last, but not least, there was Clarissa. She must have been a drill sergeant in the armed services. She informed us early on in the trip that Federal regulations prohibited the use of cell phones on the bus. Never mind the fact that we had had about four other bus drivers who never mentioned this rule. She was adamant and said if she caught anyone using their cell phone, they would be thrown off the bus! As we got into town in one station, we were actually in the downtown area and someone pulled out a cell phone to call for a ride. Man, that bus driver didn't miss a beat and told her to shut that cell phone off until they had landed in the station.

Our fellow passengers were an interesting group of people too. Most were young and many were college students. But there was one fellow on the bus dressed in an Arab robe and turban or whatever he had on his head. One fellow chattered away on his cell phone in a foreign language all the way from San Antonio to Dallas (about five hours). I was hoping he wasn't a terrorist calling ahead to the next bus station to have it blown up!

Another interesting passenger was a woman who had completely shaved her head bald except for a pony tail out the back. She traveled with us from San Antonio to Oklahoma City, she and another woman. I have to admit, I just couldn't take my eyes off of her interesting hairdo. Fortunately, she was in front of me, so my staring went unnoticed by her.

The bus stations were pretty much as the cabbie had described them. They were often in bad areas of town that I assume were in good areas of town in their inception. Some stations were worse than other - in various degrees of disrepair from the waiting rooms to the bathrooms.

Good food was rare. Most of the stations had only vending machines in them. Just a few of the major city stations had an actual lunch counter. But even in those stations, apparently, they were run by the same food service throughout the Greyhound system because you got the same thing on the menu no matter where you went. And all of it was fast food. Not at all like I remembered being able to get as a child: a nice greasy hamburger and a chocolate shake served on real dishes and glassware for under five dollars.

In Dallas, they actually had a McDonald's across the street from the bus station. We thought we had died and gone to heaven. But that McDonald's was the last good meal we had until we got to Minneapolis 14 hours later!

Sleeping on the bus was impossible as well. Since my seat didn't tilt back, I sat straight up during the night. The seat in front of me did tilt back, and that person was virtually in my lap. Since it was against the rules to put your feet out in the aisles and the seats had you packed in like sardines, all of our joints ached by morning. Tom slept fitfully with his head continually falling down in front of him. Looking around at my fellow passengers in the middle of the night, it looked like a bunch of bowling balls rolling around. Most people slept like we did – sitting up straight until your head rolled to the front or side and you woke yourself up. But there was one or two lucky people who had two seats all to themselves. Now they slept in the lap of luxury.

When we finally arrived in Minneapolis, we were to be met by a friend whom we had known about ten years ago and whom we had recently connected up with again. Because we hadn't seen him for years, we didn't really know how he had aged. Whether he would be bald or heavyset now or if he'd lost a lot of weight.

So, while waiting for him to show up, I kept looking around, wondering if this man or that man could be Dick today. I saw this one guy sitting in the waiting room where we sat. He kind of looked like our friend and he even smiled at me hopefully when I looked his way. But it turned out he was a homeless guy who hangs around the Minneapolis bus station on a regular basis!

We finally found Dick waiting for us on the outside of the station. Of course, the memory of the awful bus trip sort of faded away as we fellowshipped with our friends and attended the state fair. But I must admit that before we boarded the bus to return to San Antonio, I seriously considered taking a plane trip back! But I just hated to waste the money on the roundtrip bus fare!

SOMEBODY STOP THAT CAMPER!

This year we thought we had it made. Piece of cake! No more driving madly for three hours, spending an extra hour at our annual corn festival, and turning around to drive another three hours to get home in the wee hours of the morning so we could get to work the next day. This year, we'd combine it with a camping trip.

It was time again for the Cokato Corn Days, an event we'd traveled to quite faithfully when we lived in Minneapolis. But then it was only an hour away. Now, in Fargo, it was a full three hours away.

Though a long distance, the trip was well worth it. This county fair revolved around the town's annual free corn feed. All the farmers in town donated succulent corn on the cob, heated by a steam engine and buttered, salted, and wrapped by faithful volunteers. It was only held for three days, but all of the townspeople came and it was just a great community effort.

Annually we gorged ourselves on corn on the cob. Many people brought nine-by-thirteen-inch pans to load up as many ears as possible after standing in the long lines to the corn tent. We also partook of mini donuts, corn dogs, fried cheese curds, malts and shakes, foot-long hot dogs, French fries, and onion rings. The fair also provided rides for the children, the crowning of Miss Cokato and...you get the drift. As you can see, Tom and I go mostly for the food!

We had our trip all planned out. We would leave at noon on Tuesday, drive for three hours to a campground in the vicinity, put up our camper, and take a nap. Then we'd make a leisurely trip to Cokato, spend a few hours at the fair, drive back to our campsite, sleep for the night, and then drive home in the morning. That way we'd only miss two half-days of work.

I thought I'd help my husband, so I got the camper angled around in the garage while he was at work so that he could pull his car up to it on level ground with all four wheels on the same grade as the camper, parked. You see, in another camping trip that year, we had made the mistake of hooking up the camper to the car when the rig's back two wheels were on the level floor of the garage, but the camper's front wheel and the car were on a slanted driveway. When the camper let loose, it catapulted forward, hit the car, and bent the camper's front wheel to the tune of forty dollars!

Now, this is particularly unusual because Fargo is about the flattest city you could ever imagine. As part of the Red River Valley, it's a flat plain for fifty miles on all sides of the river. But our homebuilder built our house on higher ground in case of a flood. Thus, we have a slanted driveway on this otherwise flat land.

Anyway, I was pleased to see that I could manually push the camper around to the farthest corner of the garage and angle the car up to it so that all four wheels were on the same level as the camper wheels.

My husband attached the camper, got in the car, and attempted to leave the garage. I say "attempted" because that was all he could do. With the car at an angle, the camper at an angle, and the garage door straight, he had a crazy time trying to get out of the garage without driving over the lawn or the flowerbeds.

First, the danger was the right side: the camper might collide with the garage door. He finally got the car maneuvered so the danger was that he might hit the corner of the front porch on the left side. He could not back up either at an angle or straight, or he'd take off the left side of the garage door.

Finally, he got out of the car and unhitched the camper while I put all my weight against it so it would not fly forward and hit the car and bend the wheel again. Then we manually straightened the camper out and discovered we could push it clear to the back of the garage on one side, get the four wheels of the car on the same grade as the camper, and shoot straight out of the garage.

We were only fifteen minutes behind our scheduled departure time. Soon we were sailing down the freeway against a forty-mile-an-hour head wind. But at least we were moving toward our destination.

About two hours into the trip, I began to look at the map and read the directions to the campground where I had reserved a spot for that evening. "You know," I said, puzzled, "I can't figure out why we're traveling northeast to the campground when Cokato is southwest on the map."

"Where is the campground?" he inquired.

"Ham Lake," I replied.

"Ham Lake!" he said incredulously. "That's in St. Paul. How did you get a campground in Has Lake! That's northeast of Minneapolis!"

"Well, I just looked in the AAA book, and that was listed under Cokato," I replied. "I just assumed it was the closest campground."

Upon opening the AAA campground guide, I discovered that Ham Lake was the next town on the alphabetical list of localities in the Minnesota guide. It had nothing to do with Cokato! If we stayed at this campground, we'd be driving an hour and a half each way going back and forth to our destination.

"How could I have been so stupid!" I said.

"Don't worry," Tom said. "Let's look in the AAA book and see if there's any campgrounds that are closer, and we'll just see if we can get our money back from Ham Lake." Hence, we perused book and picked out a town called Kandiyohi that looked like it was only about thirty miles away. When we called them, they were able to accommodate us, and Tom called Ham Lake and explained our situation, and they allowed us to cancel without paying a cancellation fee.

We arrived in Kandiyohi at three thirty, a little later than we had hoped, but we still figured we could make it. After all, Cokato was only about thirty miles away now. So, we'd surely have time for our nap and be able to get to the corn festival in plenty of time. Boy, were we wrong!

The campground was about eight miles northeast of Kandiyohi on a lake. It was a beautiful area, but a bit hilly. They told us to just drive right in, choose a campsite, and come down and pay when we got situated.

We chose a great campsite that was somewhat shaded with a lovely paved drive for the camper to sit in. I suggested we park the camper right in the middle near the tree since the back of the tar area seemed to slant down a tad. So, Tom unhitched the trailer, cranked out the camper's stabilizers, and we thought we were all set to go. But then we noticed that the electrical box was about seventy-five feet from the camper. It was too long for our fifty-foot cord to reach.

We realized we were going to have to move the camper to the back of the lot. Rather than re-hitching it to the car, we decided to push it manually. We cranked up its stabilizers, put the front wheel back down, and proceeded to push it back. Tom was in the front, pushing and steering, and I was in the back so I could tell him when we had reached the end of the pavement.

As Tom started pushing it, he thought, *This isn't hard at all.* But then it began to gain momentum, and he tried to pull the camper back. When he realized he couldn't, he yelled, "Hey, get up here in the front and help me pull this thing back!"

But I was having my own problems. If you can picture a one hundred sixty-pound woman trying to stop a fifteen hundred-pound camper, you'll understand my predicament! It was gathering speed, heading down the slope behind me, which neither of us had seen before we started this maneuver. So I yelled, "We've got a problem back here." At best, I was slowing down its progress, but not by much.

All I can say is that it had to be a God-directed thought. My mind does not operate aerodynamically. But all of a sudden, I remembered what I had done in our driveway, with the garbage can caddy, to keep it from careening into the street on garbage day, and I thought, *I can turn this thing so that the wheels are at an angle and it will stop its descent.* And that is precisely what I did.

But then, as we attempted to maneuver it back up onto the pavement, we realized how steep the embankment was behind us. If I had not turned it, depending on which way it traveled, it would have either ended up in the woods or in a ravine about a half-mile down the hills. If it gathered enough speed, it could have traveled across the road into the lake!. As it dawned on us how disastrous this situation could have been, we quickly wedged logs under the wheels to keep it from rolling.

We finally got it in place, mostly on the pavement, and got the camper up. But by that time, it was too late to take a nap, and, to make matters worse, we discovered that Cokato was still a good hour away from the campground!

You know, next year I think I'll just bite the bullet and drive three hours back and forth from Fargo. At least my nerves won't be in tatters.

MEMOIRS OF A CANADIAN SKI TRIP

Words like "cozy cabins", "ski trails groomed to perfection" and "pristine wilderness" conjured up wonderful visions in my mind. As I quickly scanned the brochure for the Windy Lake Lodge, I thought this is just what we're looking for!

And the idea that we could only get to this Garden of Eden by way of a "snow train" further enthralled me. "This will be just like my dad's Canadian fishing trip where the fish were so plentiful, they all but jumped in his boat", I cried to my husband excitedly.

Though it was a bit more expensive than we'd usually pay for a weekend trip, we decided we just couldn't pass up this once-in-a-lifetime opportunity. So my husband, Tom called the resort and signed us up for the second weekend in February.

"And guess what", Tom exclaimed after getting off the phone, "this man knows about RCI timeshares too! "Naturally, I got even more excited. "I bet this will be just like our timeshare unit back in northern Minnesota!"

As the weeks got closer to our trip, we could hardly wait. We told everyone we knew about our upcoming trip. The died-in-the-wool southerners of Kentucky where we were living at the time, thought we were crazy. But some who had been up into Canada in the fall assured us we would have a marvelous time on both the train and at Windy Lake Lodge.

The day finally arrived. After our eight-hour drive to Sault Ste. Marie, we spent the night at a familiar bed and breakfast where they assured us we would have a scrumptious breakfast on the snow train on our way to Canada.

Consequently, we paid for a reduced room rate and left without breakfast.

At the train station, we got our tickets and got on the train. Most of the other passengers were snowmobilers heading further north than us to snowmobile back to Sault Ste. Marie. One other couple was traveling to Hearst at the end of the line on their anniversary. We wondered how many others were traveling to Windy Lake Lodge.

As we started our journey, we discovered, much to our chagrin, that the "scrumptious breakfast" we were promised was on another train. And the only food this train offered that any way resembled breakfast was coffee, hot chocolate and a pre-packaged bran muffin! Everyone else on the train must have known the ropes because they all sat munching happily around us, having brought lots of food in their coolers!

We had a small cooler with us, but I had nothing extra. Having packed to do our own cooking at the resort, all I had was dried oatmeal and a cold omelet! If we ate either of those, we'd be missing one of our days' breakfasts. So, we watched the scenery for the four-hour trip instead!

Finally, Mile 122 ½ arrived. As we exited the train, I noticed that we were the only people leaving. But everyone wished us well – by that time we were all one big happy family.

Upon our arrival, leis were thrown about our necks by a young man who said "Welcome to Windy Lake Lodge. This is the official welcome." I later learned that he was one of the departing guests from the previous week.

An older, quieter man took our luggage on a trailer behind his snowmobile and gave us directions to the resort. It would be about two miles and we figured, barring no wrong turns, we should get there in about a half hour.

Quickly we donned our skis and followed his snowmobile tracks to the cabins. Well, so far, the brochure was right – this was a "pristine wilderness" all right. The streams were crystal-clear, the snow drifts were six feet high, snow-laden pine trees dotted our pathway and crisp, cold air filled our nostrils. This promised to be a wonderful adventure.

After a half hour of skiing, we still seemed to be in the wilderness and began to worry that perhaps we had made a wrong turn. I started wondering if the man who took our luggage would come looking for us if we didn't show up in a reasonable amount of time or if we'd simply die out in this beautiful Canadian countryside! But just then, Tom saw the sign for the Windy Lake Lodge. As we rounded the bend and skied into camp, the hosts came out the door of their cabin and welcomed us heartily.

According to the brochure it said, "a hot lunch will be ready for you the day you arrive", but because we thought we'd eat a large breakfast on the Snow Train, we hadn't signed up for the hot lunch! With stomachs growling by this time, we followed the host to our cabin.

It was definitely a "cozy cabin". When we arrived, a roaring fire blazed in the wood burning stove. But as we listened to the host's instructions, we realized that somewhere in the brochure, we must have skipped over the most important details.

"We have no plumbing or electricity (or insulation as we could see the raw wood on the walls) in these cabins", our host explained carefully. "Your cabin is completely heated by this wood burning stove. If you let the fire go out, that box over there contains kindling and paper." What he should have said is: if you let the fire go out, you will freeze to death!

Going on with his instructions, he pointed to three containers of water, "This heated water on the wood burning stove is your face washing water, this cold water in the bucket is dish washing water and this water in the blue jug is your drinking water with a small amount of chlorine in it."

Then he instructed us on the use of our stove, a two-burner gas stove, and the propane lights. After giving us the ski map and suggesting a trail, our host left.

At that point I looked at Tom and he looked at me, and we said "well, we'll make the best of it." My positive husband assured me that "everything" would be all right and that yes, he would keep the wood burning stove going - even at night.

Up until this point in our lives, we had only had one other experience such as this to equate it to. We had stayed in a cabin in northern Minnesota in the spring that had lights, but no heat or hot water. We had rented it for a week, and ended up leaving early because Tom didn't keep the stove going at night and I was freezing most of the time.

I had visions of another weekend like that one - only worse -- I really could freeze to death up here! "Well, I'll reserve my judgment of this place until I've spent a night here," I said with much skepticism. "If I can sleep in my nightgown and not have to sleeping in every stitch of clothing I brought with me, I'll consider it a great place", I added.

After an afternoon of good skiing, we arrived ravenous at the hosts' cabin for supper. Of course, after twenty-four hours of not eating, skiing two miles into camp and then another two hours of skiing that afternoon, we'd have eaten shoe leather! But once again, like the brochure promised, it was a meal fit for a king.

But the greatest delight to us was the realization that our hosts, Tom and Shirley, were Christians! Since we were the only people at the lodge until the next day, we had time for real fellowship with them - an unusual situation, as Tom, our host explained, for his wife to be able to join us for supper. She was usually tied to the kitchen having to serve everyone.

50

So sweet was our fellowship that the time passed quickly that evening. Before we knew it, three hours had gone by and it was time to retire.

Before leaving, I told our hosts that I was going to treat this like a camping trip and not drink too many fluids in the evening, since the latrine was quite a ways from our cabin. I could envision a 2:00 a.m. trek in the pitch black Canadian night amongst the night creatures!

"Oh", Shirley exclaimed, "we have a chamber pot for you to take to your cabin at night." I was so thrilled – you'd think this woman had offered me the Gutenberg Bible! Giddy with delight, I clutched my roll of toilet paper and chamber pot and hiked to my cabin. It's funny how, having lowered my sights, I could appreciate much simpler solutions!

As we got ready for bed, I thought longingly, however, of how good a nice hot bath would feel. Then the Lord gave me the brilliant idea to at least soak our feet in hot water before jumping into bed! What a difference even that made.

As I climbed into the cold bed, I again remembered with a pang how much I depended on our flannel sheets and electric blanket to warm me. Though the sheets were cold, Tom assured me that he would keep me warm. I've always said he is like a human heater. God must have turned the flame up on that man when He created him.

We went to sleep that night laying like two spoons. When he rolled over, I rolled over and vice versa. As we drifted off to sleep, I said, "if we should freeze to death, they'd have to make an awfully odd-shaped coffin to put us in." I assumed rigor mortis would set in before anyone found us, and they wouldn't be able to pry us apart, much less straighten us out! But my beloved husband was true to his word about keeping the fire going in the cabin. Every three hours, he got up and added another log to the stove. Then, in the early morning, he opened the damper to let more heat into the cabin.

Our first breakfast was supposed to be an omelet that I could warm in the microwave! I had pre-cooked it and I was at a loss as to how to operate without a microwave. But then the Lord gave me the idea to warm it in a pan on top of the wood burning stove – which we did, and it heated it just enough to get hot without scorching it as it would have on an open flame.

However, after skiing about three hours that day and a bit more bravery on my part (since I was getting to know the hosts a little better), I asked Tom if he'd go buy six crackers and a slab of peanut butter from Shirley. But to my delight, she invited us in for lunch with the latest arrivals. I tell you, soup never tasted so good!

Over the next couple of days, we experienced more great ski trails. They lived up to the description in the brochure too. And in the evening, we headed back to our hosts' cabin for more of Shirley's wonderful cooking, followed by games with other guests.

By the last day, we found ourselves reluctant to leave. Waiting at the train stop, I thought with a pang, "I don't want to leave this place. I feel like I've been in an incubator and now I am about to be expelled back into the cold, busy, cruel world." I thought seriously of asking the hosts if we could stay on for the week. But of course, like James, John and Peter in the Bible who wanted to stay on the mountaintop with Jesus at the transfiguration, I too had to get back into the world.

But our experience at Windy Lake Lodge was so marvelous that we knew it would forever change our lives. For the next several days we kept comparing our timeshare unit with all the amenities to the love and nurturing we had received through our hosts at Windy Lake Lodge, and realized that nothing the world gives us can replace loving relationships!

BACK ON THE ROAD AGAIN

Florida was our favorite state in America. This time we were driving down from MN and planning to be there for two whole weeks. The first week we were staying at a timeshare and the second week we would travel around the southern regions of the state. Our plan was to travel through the Everglades, stay near Miami, and then out to the Keys where we would go camping. I wanted to swim in the ocean at the very end of the United States.

Our first week in the timeshare gave us the time we needed to unwind. Then after leaving our timeshare, we began our travels as we headed down towards Miami. Unfortunately, we reached the Everglades at night. I just prayed we wouldn't have car trouble and have to spend the night out with the alligators. I do admit to losing my flexibility a bit here. I was mad at Tom for not getting us through this area and to a hotel before nightfall.

Finally, about 11 o'clock at night, I was sleepy as well as mad and inflexible, and I insisted that Tom stop somewhere in the nearest town. We happened to be out near the airport in Miami at that point, so he took the first hotel we could find.

It was definitely a bit seedy. There were bars on the windows and the sheets must have been a bargain bought from a now defunct state hospital that was stamped on them. And the clientele at the hotel was a lot of prostitutes coming in at all hours of the night, I guess, after a hard night's work.

After a good night's sleep, while I was packing us up to go for the next leg of our trip, I sent my husband outside to take a picture of our hotel, as we often did on vacations. He said while he was snapping pictures of it, some man walked up to him and said, "Nice hotel, huh?"

The next day would find us driving through the Keys. About midday we made it to the last Key and found the state park and set up our tent. The wind was really strong and we could barely hang onto our tent flaps when we were erecting it. But we finally got it set up. And then we decided to go into town for supper. Usually we cook onsite when camping, but since we were only going to stay overnight, we hadn't purchased groceries.

When we got back after supper, it was still windy out and we decided rather than start a fire, we would just turn in. In the middle of the night, though, I awakened and had to go to the rest room. By that time the wind had died down.

When I left the tent, it never occurred to me to zip the tent back up. Tom said as soon as I left, because it was no longer windy, every mosquito in the state park must have realized that "supper" was being served in our tent. When I came back from the latrine, Tom was slapping himself silly trying to get rid of the mosquitoes. I entered and re-zipped, but by then it was too late. The tent was filled with mosquitoes. You know that sound they make and then stop, you know darn well that they've landed on someone on some exposed place on your body, but you're not sure where.

Finally, after being unsuccessful at killing them and sleep now eluding us, we decided to get up and take down our tent and leave. We did more of a roll up of our equipment than our usual neat way of packing away the tent – partly because of the time of night and partly because of the mosquitoes. But finally, Tom was ready to get the car turned around, so we could head out. "Now, Tom," I warned him, "Whatever you do, don't put on your headlights. It's four in the morning and the people in the tents aren't going to appreciate seeing your headlights in the middle of the night." I knew how thin the material was on those tent walls.

So Tom, like the good listener he was, promptly put on his headlights. In fact, it almost looked like he had his brights on! Quickly, though, we slunk out of the campground and headed back through the Keys to southern Florida.

Our next stop was going to be Kissimee, Florida just outside of Disney World. We had reservations at the Bass Lake Campground. Unfortunately, we arrived at this one late at night as well. And of course there were hardly any campsites left.

When we went in to register, the clerk told us that we could camp on a spot right by the rest rooms! "Oh, great," I thought. Then he told us we needed to pay him a deposit of five dollars to use the rest room. I looked at him and said, "You mean I have to pay five dollars just to go to the bathroom???" And he looked at me and said in his southern drawl, "You mean you don't ha-ave five dollars? We went back and forth on that one for a bit until finally I realized that the five-dollar fee was a deposit to ensure that I didn't trash the bathroom while we were camping there and that I would get the five dollars back at the end of my stay.

We did attempt to set up our tent on this spot by the rest rooms, we really did, but I kept getting bitten on my feet. I didn't know what it was, but later found out they were fire ants. For some reason, Tom never got bit.

Finally, we just gave up trying to get a tent up and decided to sleep in the back of our station wagon. But by the time we were ready to doze off, the night was very still and it was beyond warm in the car. We tried to open our windows, but it being muggy in Kissimmee, just like in the Keys, an open window was an open invitation to the mosquitoes. So, all night long we were opening and closing the window between sleeping fitfully.

The other issue was that we were also very near the water tower for the campground. And all night long we heard the water tower pumping the water. It turned out to be a very sleepless night. Actually, it turned out to be kind of a sleepless trip too, due to our adventures through the Everglades at eleven p.m. and our wild time camping in the Keys. The last decent sleep we had was in the timeshare the previous week.

STRETCHING EXERCISES

If there's one thing I have learned in life – the hard way, I might add – it is that when you are going into a new situation, let your expectations go and be willing to be flexible. I say I have learned this the hard way because after being on this earth for fifty-something years and having been a Christian for thirty-five of those years, I still walk into what could be great adventures with my expectations fully intact.

A prime example is the mini retreat my husband, Tom, and I decided to take just this past weekend. We were very tired physically and emotionally, and just felt like we needed a getaway. Not having tried any of the Bed & Breakfasts in North Dakota yet, we decided to try one in Luverne.

The B&B on the Internet ad sounded like it was right up our alley: a 300-acre farm where you could rest, watch birds, hike, and even canoe nearby if you so desired. The weekend weather promised to be just perfect.

So we set off: Tom, I, and our dog, Joyful. The dog's mini retreat, although she would be able to go with us on our excursions, would be spent sleeping in the back of our station wagon.

Our first mistake was that I directed Tom on some back roads on what appeared to me to be a shortcut to Luverne. But I should have remembered from a sermon I heard once that shortcuts only look short on the surface; they usually end up being longer or tougher than one anticipates.

And such was this road. Traditionally in North Dakota, they don't pave roads until they need them for heavier traffic. This one didn't look like they would have that problem anytime soon! After the pavement left us and we had traveled for several miles on a road that assured us you could travel at fifty miles an hour, which we were never able to get above forty due to the loose gravel, my husband finally gave me one of those looks that told me he wasn't a happy camper at this point. He hates washboard roads, dusty roads, and stones that fly back and hit the car. I looked at him and shrugged my shoulders and said, "I'm sorry, I didn't know".

Finally, after about fifteen miles, we arrived at the Bolden Farm Bed & Breakfast. But no one was home. The house was unlocked, and we walked throughout the house calling "hello", to which no one answered. I couldn't remember whether the hostess had asked what time we were coming, if there was a check-in time or if I had said what time we would be arriving. So, in an effort to be flexible, we took our reading material out onto the front porch and read in a couple of wicker chairs until we finally dozed off to sleep.

An hour and ten minutes went by, and the comfort of the wicker chair for a bed was losing its flavor. It was one of those fitful sleeps where you doze off until your head falls down, and then you suddenly wake up again. Finally, we decided to take our suitcase in the house and see if we couldn't find the north bedroom, which was what I thought she told me on the phone she was going to put us in.

But at that point, our hostess finally arrived home. She asked us gaily if we were the Girlings, and we told her no, we were the Hladys. She said, "Oh, I didn't expect you until six o'clock!"

Nevertheless, she got us settled in the right room. Even at that point, my expectations were getting in my way. It was a small room with only a double bed. I kept comparing it to other B&Bs that had big, spacious rooms with queen-sized beds. But I tried to delight in the things here.

We finally did get a nap in, but the bed was another surprise. It was as hard as a rock. It felt like we were sleeping on a cement slab. I kept wondering if someone was going to prepare me for my burial soon!

That evening we asked our hostess where she would recommend us to go for supper. Cooperstown was fifteen miles away and promised a couple of restaurants, Valley City was 35 miles away and according to our hostess, had all the restaurants you could ever hope to find, but Luverne was only about five miles away and had a place called Rockin' Rodney's which was a bar and grill, but she promised us they had hand-pattied hamburgers and steaks and ribs and walleye that would melt in your mouth.

Being still exhausted, we decided to go to Rockin' Rodney's. It was definitely a one-horse town. It had a handful of houses and Rockin' Rodney's. It had no gas stations or grocery stores. In fact they barely had a "welcome to Luverne" sign.

But we were hungry and tired, so we pulled up to the restaurant and walked in. Right away I could see that we were overdressed. I was in a dress and Tom had changed into a pair of nice slacks and a golf shirt. And the rest of the folks in the restaurant were all in jeans and T-shirts.

As soon as we sat down and she didn't bring us a menu, I had a feeling this wasn't the night for all the great fixin's. And I was right. The waitress arrived at our table and said "What'll it be, folks? Our specials tonight are pizza or Taco fry bread." Not wanting to hurt the waitress' feelings by getting up and leaving, Tom, in his attempt to be flexible, asked about the pizza. To which she replied "Oh, it's just a frozen pizza that we throw in the microwave." We both ordered the taco fry bread and two cokes.

It wasn't too bad, but I must admit that I was grumbling something about my "rights" on vacations inside my mind. But we both tried to make each other think we were having a great first night of our vacation. At the end of the meal, my husband asked the waitress what that delicious fry bread was. And she said "oh, it's just frozen bread dough that we throw in the deep fryer"! Somehow I didn't think she would be getting the Waitress Of The Month award this time around. But our bill was a real shocker: Fourteen dollars! I figured the cokes alone probably were about three dollars apiece. And then my husband, in his generous spirit, decided to leave Ms. Personality a three-dollar tip!

Being a bit disappointed in our supper, Tom suggested we drive into Valley City for ice cream. On the back roads, it took us about forty-five minutes to get there. We found that Valley City wasn't all it was cracked up to be either. Perhaps we had entered the city on the wrong road, but I didn't see all the restaurants that our hostess told us about. We thankfully found a Dairy Queen where we stopped for a blizzard. Then since it was beginning to get dark, we decided to try to find our way home.

Unfortunately we had left the directions to her B&B back in our room. My old eyes had difficulty seeing the map in the dark and so we just tried to head in a northwesterly direction. Narrow country roads in North Dakota can seem pretty desolate – especially when there is no other traffic and apparently no habitation.

At one point Tom was looking over at a cemetery on his side of the road when his wheels began to veer off the right shoulder where there was about an inch of grass for the shoulder before it dipped down into a dropoff. My nerves were frayed by that time and I literally shouted at him,"Please keep your eyes on the road. I do not want to roll this car over in a place where we probably wouldn't be found for days by anybody!" He was kind enough to hold his silence and get back on the roadway.

Finally shortly after ten o'clock in the dark of night we found our way back to the B&B. Thankfully our hostess was waiting up for us.

Before retiring, we decided to take a nice hot bath in the clawfoot bathtub. That was one of those special things I always looked forward to at B&B's we'd stayed at in the past. I turned on the hot water in the spacious bathroom and let it run while I got ready for my bath. Five minutes later I checked the water only to find out that it was still cold.

I called Tom at that point and said maybe they got the faucets switched. So he came in and tried turning on the cold faucet. But five minutes later it was still cold. So he turned the hot water back on and said he was beginning to feel a difference. Of course Tom is the kind of guy that can take an Asprin and five minutes later "feel better already"!

The spigot was another interesting situation. It was so narrow that just a hard jet of water shot out. But as the tub began to fill, I decided to get in in faith. Thankfully, I took a book with me so that I wouldn't get bored while I waited for the tub to fill.

Finally I began to feel the warm water rising around me - about a half hour later. But I soon realized this tub must have been made for a midget. Try as I might, I couldn't submerge my knees beneath the water. Being a tall person, I have long legs. Stretched out in this tub with my back flat against the back of the tub and my feet flat against the front of the tub, to my chagrin, my knees were still bent! I tried turning to one side or the other to get my knees wet, but it was to no avail. The only way I could dampen my knees was to splash water on them and then I had to keep doing so periodically since they kept getting cold. I know, I know, I was trying to be flexible. Tom had the same problems, but he seemed to have a better attitude about it than I did.

After a sound sleep on the cement slab and awakening to the sunshine, our outlook was brighter for the next day. We got to know our hostess a bit and ate a scrumptious breakfast, and we were ready to see what the day had in store for us.

We decided for our first excursion to go on a three-mile hike that our hostess said would be easy. Well, I don't know if we got our directions wrong – I admit that our hostess talked fast and waved her arms a lot pointing in different directions and of course she knew the countryside. We didn't want to appear dumb, so we set off in the direction we thought she told us to go. But it soon became clear that we weren't sure which way to go.

I remembered her mentioning a creek to us that would take us out to the road. The creek appeared to be about three stories down a very steep hill. Wanting to be good sports, we climbed down the hill to the creek. But the creek path wasn't exactly a walk in the park. If you walked near the creek, there were tree roots, rocks and other asundry to scale. If you went up the opposite hillside a bit, you were walking on a slant.

Several times I asked Tom if he was sure this was the right way. "Trust me" he kept saying. Finally I said "if we don't get to that road in fifteen minutes, I'm backtracking". Fifteen minutes later we were heading home the same way we came.

When we arrived back at the B&B, our hostess assured us we were on the right path and would have come out to the road eventually. But I was pretty sure nobody had been on that trail for several centuries. Not to be daunted by one bad experience, we decided to go on a canoe trip that our hostess assured us would take us only three hours at the most. After all, what could happen in a canoe?

The plan was that our hostess was going to drive us to the Bible Camp where we would rent a canoe, she would give us her cell phone and we would call her when we arrived at the bridge and she would come down and pick us and the canoe up at the bridge. However, when we got back from our hike, she informed us that she had gotten bitten by something while working out in the garden and had taken two Benadryl to ensure that the bite wouldn't affect her.

Well, I knew about Benadryl. It puts you out like a light! She must have known that too, but she insisted we take her pickup truck and leave it at the bridge and she would go home and rest, and that way we would have wheels to get back to the Bible camp and back to the B&B.

Somehow or another we must have given her the impression that we were expert canoeists. We realized this when she was talking to the camp director as he was helping us get our gear together. As we pushed off from shore with our dog, Joyful in the middle of the canoe, I was just praying that we wouldn't tip it over in front of them!

We did make it out to the middle of the stream after a bit of maneuvering and Tom giving me instructions from the back. The only problem we had in getting started was that our dog kept shifting positions in the canoe and every time she did, the canoe would tilt to one side or the other.

Soon we were paddling like pros down the stream. When I saw an object ahead of us, I'd call out "right rudder" or "left rudder". When my arm got tired on one side, I'd call out "switch sides". We were a great team.

After about a half an hour we decided to stop for lunch. Our gracious hostess had packed some sandwiches and fruit for us in a cooler. But with the tippiness of the canoe and the dog in the middle, we decided it would be best to find someplace to stop along the way.

Well, that was easier said than done. While other rivers have sand bars, North Dakota has mud bars! The first place we stopped, I put my foot out in the muddy embankment and it disappeared from view. I thought maybe we had hit quick sand! Finally we realized that due to the North Dakota soil, which was like black clay, and the recent rains they had had, this was all we were going to find for a river embankment.

We did eventually find a place where the clay was harder and we were able to land the canoe, pull it up and secure it. We ate our lunch in a cow pasture, dipped our dog in the river and were soon on our way again.

Our hostess assured us that we would pass under two bridges on our journey, but it was the second one that would be our destination. After a couple of hours, we were going under the first bridge.

To our credit, I must say that we did not drift a great deal. We kept paddling steadily. But it soon became apparent that we were not in shape for a three-hour trip. Two hours, yes. Three hours, no.

We had also not prepared well for this trip. It was a bright sunny day and we had no sun block on and Tom had no cap on, and it was obvious this trip was taking longer than it should have.

The last two hours we hit a southern head wind. It was so strong that we dared not stop paddling to rest our arms or we would drift backward. In the wind, we were lucky if we were going two miles an hour.

I began to quote Bible verses to myself to keep my spirits up. Around every bend we hoped to see our bridge. But around every bend was more water and more wind. The dog was moaning probably from boredom and being uncomfortable in the canoe, the deer flies were biting us fiercely, we were sunburned, our lips were parched from lack of water and both of us were sore from sitting in one position in the canoe for so long. And to make matters worse, the shoreline was nothing but reeds. It was hard to tell which direction to go – whether you were headed for a bay or continuing downstream. And there was no place to pull the canoe out and get on shore even to stand up for a few minutes.

Even once we saw the bridge, it was about three more bends in the river around the reeds before we got to it. It's a good thing it was the right bridge, because we were so worn out that we were both crying out to the Lord by that time out loud, begging Him to get us to someplace where we could stop. We were prepared to find a farmer and call our hostess from a farmhouse. We didn't care if we had to have a helicopter come pick us up. The goal no longer mattered. It was survival that we were after.

The canoe trip that should have taken us three hours took us four hours. When we finally arrived at our destination, we pulled the canoe up on some rocks that were part of the underneath side of the bridge. Then we had to pull the canoe up a steep embankment. My husband said it looked like nobody had pulled their canoe out of the water at this bridge for years!

Tom went and got the pickup truck so that he could pull it as close to the river as he could. We finally got the canoe maneuvered into the pickup, but because it was a mini pickup, over half the canoe stuck out the back end! We were afraid we would lose it on the way back to the Bible camp, so it was decided that the dog would ride inside the cab with him and I would ride in the back of the truck so that I could hang onto the canoe as we bumped over the gravel roads.

We did make it safely back to the camp without mishap. And the rest of the time at the B&B was definitely more restful. We decided not to attempt any more adventures, but just stay sedentary for the rest of the weekend.

And I must admit, that as I laid on the cement slab that second night, it didn't seem as hard as it had the first night. As I pondered all that we had gone brought through that weekend, I concluded that maybe there is still hope that I can change me into a more flexible person.

WHOA, WILBUR

Now, you must understand that though I am a dog person, I know next to nothing about horses. I never grew up around them, I never enjoyed drawing them in art class and the few times I ever rode one, it left my nerves definitely jangled. Unlike others, I knew, the experience of flying through the fields on a gallop filled me with sheer terror.

My husband, on the other hand, had constantly regaled me from the very start of our marriage with stories about his brother's horse, Rex, who he claimed was like a big friendly dog. And when Tom would visit his brother's farm and call Rex's name, Rex would come running to Tom from way across the fields. "Oh," he said, "Rex rode like a Cadillac". When he was on Rex, he felt like he and the horse were one!

This is why his sudden loss of memory really surprised me. You see, we were up in Brainerd, MN cross country skiing in January one year. There is nothing better than the county and state trails in this part of MN for skiing. Some of the trails are groomed and some are not. But it really doesn't matter. The trails are long and hilly, they go through various types of terrain: heavily wooded, open fields, nice long gentle slopes and some hills that take your breath away.

We decided this day to visit the Cut Lake trails just about 30 miles north of Brainerd. But when we arrived, much to our surprise, we discovered that they had turned the entire park (not just a portion of the trails, but the whole park) into ski skating trails! We and several other skiers were flabbergasted. What had they done to our beautiful park?

Ski skating had become the rage in MN, and it was not at all compatible with traditional cross country skiers. They need wide paths and have edges on their skies which they use to ski in a skating motion on the paths. Traditional cross-country skiers need a groomed trail. Their feet stay glued firmly to the trails, going both up and down them. The only time ski skaters keep their feet glued to the trails is when they are coming down a hill. Otherwise, it's all about the exercise!

I tended to look at ski skaters about the same way I looked at the bikers who wore those skin-tight shorts, skin tight shirts and helmets. They looked like insects from outer space who took no time to smell the roses, just zipped through them at a high rate of speed.

So we began asking around: where else can we find a traditional cross country ski park that is groomed? Well, the nearest one was in Hackensack, MN, which was about forty-five minutes up the road. Since we were on vacation, we decided to go for it.

We had been on the road for about fifteen minutes and had just gone through a town when we began to see this horse galloping alongside the pavement. The horse seemed to be lost and frantic.

As I said, I am not a horse person, but I could see he was running in blind terror. So I turned to Tom and said, "We've got to stop that horse." I said, "You know horses, what do we do?" He looked at me and said, "I don't know anything about horses!"

My mouth hung open, but due to the demise of the horse, I wasn't about to start reminding him about he and Rex being "one" when they rode. So I said, "pull over in front of it", (since it was running on our side of the road at that point). Tom pulled over in front of the horse, but the horse just ran on around and past the car and on to the other side of the road. But then he stood stock still for a moment.

I got out of the car, well remembering what they used to do in the old westerns, and said with my most commanding voice: "Whoa". And lo and behold, the horse stopped his frantic motions and looked at me.

I continued walking over to him, bolstered by his response to me, saying, "easy, boy, easy, boy" – just like I heard the cowboys in those old westerns say when they were trying to tame a wild horse. At that point, I had visions of myself in a cowgirl outfit, complete with the hat.

Getting over finally to his side of the road, I was able to take the reins, pat him on the mane and walk him back towards town with Tom trailing in the car.

As we neared town, we were looking for a place to drop him off so that we could be on our way skiing in Hackensack. Eventually we saw some type of store that sold trailers and whatnot that had a fenced in area. But when we approached the owner outside, he just said, "You're not dumping that horse off on me!" I don't know if he thought I should take him home with me or what!

But I thought it was pretty obvious that the horse wasn't mine. I'm dressed in my cross-country ski clothes and boots. Can't this guy see that I'm just a dumb tourist who happened upon a stray horse!

So while the owner and another man stood there debating the issue, along comes a police car. He also left me standing by the side of the road holding the horse while he discussed with the other two gentlemen the issue of the horse. Apparently a whole herd of horses had escaped from a local farmer's barn.

You would have thought I was invisible the way the policeman and the two local guys treated me. The policeman tried to locate the owner who was in a meeting at his place of business and couldn't be disturbed, but then stayed parked by the side of the road. The two local guys at the store kept discussing the situation with the horses escaping and how if they didn't pass a new local law, it meant that the town was going to have to deal with a lot more of this type of stuff from now and. And me? I just continued to stand there next to my horse.

Finally a blue collar worker joined the two store guys and turned to me and said, you shouldn't have to get in the middle of this (at last somebody noticed me!). "Bring that horse over here to this yard and you can be on your way."

YOU'RE OFF THE MAP!

My idea of being relaxed on a vacation is putting your watch on upside down and not noticing for several hours or having nothing more important to do than clipping your toenails because you've neglected it for the past several months because you were too busy working! A relaxing vacation is *not* discovering that your husband left both his Daytimer (with the trip itinerary) and your Traveler's checks at home on the counter!

Though I was really upset at Tom for these misdemeanors, we arrived in Fort Myers, Florida for a two-week vacation, which we both badly needed, safe and sound. We'd driven from Fargo to Minneapolis four hours one way the day before, the hotel assuring us that they would watch our car while we were on our trip. You see, we'd gotten these great deals on Air Trans, but you had to fly out of Minneapolis and you had to fly out in the middle of the week and then come home in the middle of the week. It seemed that every day it was a different price. Since we wanted to save money, we decided to go with the program.

From Fort Myers, we followed our Map Quest directions to St. Petersburg where we were spending the first three days before our timeshare week in Fort Myers Beach. But I came to the conclusion that getting off the plane and traveling two to three hours by car to get to your destination on the first day of a vacation is not a good idea. I, unfortunately, being the perfectionist I am, cannot let something go, and when I discovered Tom left the two aforementioned items at home, I'm afraid I ragged on him for most of the trip up the coast.

Map Quest is not always the most reliable source of directions. Sometimes it takes you way out of the way to get you to your destination. I've wondered if they don't promise the local merchants that they will do that on purpose so that you see more of the fine city you are visiting. Such was our trip to St. Petersburg. It should have only taken us two hours if we had taken the directions that the hotel owner had given us – but of course those directions were back home in the Daytimer!!! Finally, we arrived though.

I had booked this hotel on the Internet about five months earlier. The month before we were due to arrive, Bruce, the hotel owner, wrote me and said they were sorry, but they had inadvertently overbooked and would we mind staying in a three-bedroom house for the same price as our one-bedroom efficiency would have been, but it was four blocks from the beach. (I kept wondering who got their reservation in first – surely the other guy couldn't have booked before we did!). But we agreed that we would stay the two nights in the efficiency and then move so he could accommodate the other guest.

But then Bruce wrote back and said, "Well, we were hoping you'd want to stay in the house all three nights. After all, it's double the work for us to have to clean two units." But Tom and I had our hearts set on being on the beach. So I wrote back again and said, "how about if we cut a deal. I will gladly do the housecleaning in both places if we can just stay on the beach for the first two nights. We spent our honeymoon in that area and haven't been back for several years, couldn't we please, please, please stay on the beach?"

Bruce wrote back, misunderstanding what I was trying to get across, and said, "we've made an executive decision, we've decided that we don't want to break up your anniversary, so we're putting you in "The Rabbit Hutch", a freestanding cottage with a fully equipped kitchen on our motel property at the same price and you can stay there for all three nights! I hadn't meant to misrepresent myself, but somehow he thought it was our anniversary. At that point I was just too tired to fight it any longer and decided to take it. But I was determined to let him know when we got there that it really wasn't our anniversary – I didn't want him to think I had lied to him.

The Rabbit Hutch was about a 1950's style bright pink cottage, but it had 1990's furniture in it, which means that it had small rooms and big furniture. In fact the furniture was so large that you had to walk sideways around the beds and two people could not be in the room at the same time!

There was a queen-sized bed in our room, but by the looks of the two bed lamps on one of the other walls, I'd say that back in the 1950's, there had probably been twin beds (like in I Love Lucy) in there. Now there was no other furniture except for this overly large bed. When you read at night, you had to do so by the overhead light since there was no room for nightstands and lamps. We tried, without success, to move the dresser lamp from the other bedroom, but discovered it was bolted to the dresser. We were able, however, to move a clock – it was the only thing not bolted down – and set it on top of one of the opposite wall lamps so we could see its dial at night.

One of the benefits of staying at this hotel were the extras they allotted you. Free of charge, you could take beach chairs and umbrellas to the beach across the street as well as bicycles for use.

The unfortunate thing about The Rabbit Hutch is that because it was freestanding, everybody thought it was the office. Tom, earlier on the plane, had asked me what was the first thing I was going to do when I arrived at the cottage. I told him I was going to take a nap. So I got into my nightgown shortly after our arrival.

While Tom was talking on the phone to the bank at home about our "lost" Traveler's checks, a couple of ladies knocked on the door. Since we had never seen the owner's wife, Tom thought these two ladies were the owner's wife and someone else.

As I lay on the bed reading in the other room, he came to the bedroom door and announced that there were a couple of ladies to see me. "Oh, no," I thought, "I can't go out there in my nightgown." But being as tired as I was, I decided to fake it. So I promptly went into the living room and explained that I was in my nightgown because I was going to take a nap. At which point the two ladies asked to see their room! I think they were as embarrassed as I was once they realized that our cottage wasn't the renting office!

The second day Tom decided we should take a bike ride down Gulf Boulevard to a restaurant he remembered from our trip there seven years ago. It was called The Friendly Fisherman and Tom assured me he thought it was maybe five miles at the most. It's true that we hadn't ridden bikes for five years, but we worked out at the Y regularly on the treadmill. I figured it may take a little to get our sea legs back, but it couldn't be that bad. And look at the gas we'd save not using the car!

Well, the five-mile bike ride, as usual with Tom, turned out to be a lot longer than he had guessed. As we later discovered, we traveled twenty miles roundtrip! But the worst thing was the bicycle Tom had "chosen" for me. I guess he chose this one because it was a girl's bike, but the seat was as hard as a rock and I couldn't remember if fifth gear was high speed or low speed. So I put it in third gear, but even at that speed, I felt like I was pedaling down the road pushing a steam shovel.

Perhaps it was because the wind was against us or because I was twenty pounds overweight or because I hadn't ridden in so long, but Tom was just flying along. Periodically I would try to pedal faster to keep up and accomplish it, but then fall behind again. Then I gave up and decided if I just tried to keep sight of his yellow shirt a quarter mile up the road, we should make it there at least in the same day. At one point when he stopped to wait for me, I asked him how much farther he thought it was and he said "oh, about a couple miles". Then within minutes we saw a sign that said Indian Rocks Beach was another four miles!

Finally we stopped some locals, and when they heard where we were headed, told us that restaurant was just for the tourists, that we should just go on another couple of miles and eat at a place called Dave's Dock where they had the best grouper sandwich on the gulf.

Well, at that point I didn't think I could go another two feet let alone five miles, no matter how great the grouper sandwich was, so I suggested we turn around and head home. Tom kindly suggested I take his faster bike with the softer seat and he took mine. We did finally find a restaurant on the way home and the meal was great and they were the ones who told us how many miles we had actually traversed.

The joy of our trip was the time we spent on the beach. However, it also turned out to be some of the most harrowing experiences in our trip. The first day we went to the beach, we sighted a manatee about an eighth of a mile out. Several people were following it while walking along the beach. It was huge. But unbeknownst to me, while we were out swimming and floating in the saltwater, Tom spied another one about twnety feet from me. He didn't want to frighten me as he knew it surely would, so he gently suggested that we make our way in to shore. Then on dry land, he told me about it. Manatees are supposed to be like big gentle cows, but to him, it looked like a baby whale.

At another point in the trip when we were also swimming in the ocean about 40 yards out, I suddenly looked behind Tom and saw a black fin sticking up about a foot and a half in the air. It was in closer to shore than we were! I yelled at Tom,

"Look out, look out. There's a shark!" He looked at me, assuming I was pulling his leg because of the incident with the manatee and said "what, what?" But apparently the look on my face must have convinced him because he looked over his shoulder and saw the black fin too and yelled " swim for shore". So we swam like the dickens. Safely on shore, Tom said, "as if we could outswim a shark!"

There were several people swimming at the beach that day. Apparently we were the only ones to see it until it surfaced again a few seconds later out quite a ways farther out in the ocean. Then you should have seen the folks up the beach leave the water!

This was also a trip for getting lost. On our way down to Fort Myers Beach, we decided to stop in Sarasota because I have a niece living there. I hadn't told her I was coming, but wanted to surprise her and just show up on her doorstep. We got the address and then began asking townspeople how to get to her house. It seemed like every gas station we stopped at, we'd either find people who could speak very little English or they had just moved there and didn't have a clue where we were or where we wanted to go.

But in Sarasota, one customer in a gas station gave us directions. But somehow or other we kept getting turned around. We bought a city map, but when I thought we were heading south, we were heading north. Finally we stopped at a garden store on the outskirts of town and asked them to show us where we were on the map. The man looked at me and said, "Lady, you aren't even *on* the map! You're way up here!"

After wandering around for two hours, we finally decided we'd just have to leave without finding Ann. After all, she wasn't expecting us, so she'd never know we had tried to find her.

Finding our resort was an interesting trip as well. It was listed as Fort Myers, but when we started asking the locals where Fisherman's Village was, they'd never heard of it. Finally we called information and reached the resort and discovered it was twenty miles up the road we had just traveled on in a town called Punta Gorda! We finally found the resort, but then had major difficulty finding our unit.

After checking in, the lady at the timeshare office gave us a map of the Village and pointed out where number forty-five was. It looked pretty easy to find, so Tom did something he has never done before and probably will never do again, he gave me the key and said, "Here, you go find our unit and I'll be along shortly with the luggage."

What the lady failed to tell us was that Fisherman's Village was a high class shopping area with the timeshare units on the second floor. She also failed to tell us that you couldn't drive your car all the way down to the unit because the parking lot didn't go that far.

I discovered that the units were up on the second floor, but after twenty minutes of waiting for Tom, I finally gave up and went back to the office and told the lady I had lost my husband and if he stopped back here, would she please send him to the unit.

In the meantime, Tom was on the back side of nowhere. Discovering quite early that he couldn't drive down to the unit, he decided to make several trips (seven, to be exact) between the car and the unit. Rolling one of the suitcases through gravel and various other interesting terrain, he got down to number forty-five on the lower level, saw what looked like a balcony (never mind the fact that it was about two and a half feet wide with peeling paint on it and no sides) outside of a sliding glass door and assumed that must be the unit.

(I later asked him how he could possibly mistake this for a balcony, which definitely wasn't handicap accessible when it had no railing on it and was not even wide enough for two people to stand on side by side, and he said he assumed that the manager knew we weren't handicapped, so they put us in this unit!)

The stairs up to the "balcony" looked like something on a ship that a Stevadore would go up! There were about three steps at an angle. It actually looked more like a slanted ladder and the steps were about ten inches apart vertically and didn't meet each other horizontally, but were staggered. Tom dragged the suitcase (the one that felt like it had gold bricks in it) up this ladder, set it down on the balcony and pounded on the sliding glass door. When no one answered, he decided to make the other six trips. Each time he arrived back at the condo, he'd pound on the door again. He said he could see people inside, but no one would answer the door! And he definitely couldn't see me.

Finally, abandoning the luggage on the balcony outside the door, he went back down to the office to confront the manager and inform her that she had sent him to the wrong unit. But she quickly assured him that I was in the unit and waiting for him, and would send a security guard with him to show him where the unit was. Then she called me and said "we have your husband down at the office and will be sending him up shortly". I couldn't help but wonder if she thought he was on a day pass from a local nursing home!

But faithful to her word, Tom and I were re-united 40 minutes after our arrival.

The resort also had quite colorful clientele. Aside from the thirteen stray cats living in the open air village below us waiting for fish scraps, at our end of the units were a couple restaurants and a bar called Harpoon Harry's. We soon discovered that this was the local stopping place for all the motorcycle gangs going through town. The problem was it was a one-way direction to the bar and then they had to leave on a one-way direction under our balcony. At two a.m. you'd hear the motorcycles revving up their motors, feeling good after the evening's libations and then peeling out en masse underneath our unit!

Another excursion we went on was in Arcadia, Florida, a small town about 30 miles from Fort Myers Beach where we wanted to buy oranges to take back home with us. It was advertised that there was a fruit stand there, but when we arrived in town and began inquiring about the fruit stand, no one seemed to know what we were talking about. Some even said it had burned down a few years back. But we were determined to find one, so we finally ended up at the public library (the police station was going to be my next stop) and they directed us out of town to Joshua Citrus Orchard. Well, I shouldn't say really "directed us". There were two older women trying to give us directions and both were giving us a little different directions and arguing with each other over how to get there.

Needless to say, we finally found the orchard and decided to get two large bags of oranges because they were two for one! We mistakenly thought we could send them on the airplane with our luggage! But when we got to the airport, we were informed that it would cost us fifteen dollars apiece to put these bags of oranges with our luggage (the bags of oranges themselves only cost ten dollars apiece), and so we ended up carrying them through several airports.

But truly the highlight of our trip was the golf game on Sanibel Island. The island was an exclusive little nugget that you paid an arm and a leg to even cross to from the mainland. But let me back up a bit.

Before the trip, a friend told Tom how to get discount rates for golf in FL. Through this website, Tom was able to pay half of what it would have cost us. Then we debated whether or not to take our clubs, but decided to see if we could find a local place to deliver clubs for us. And before we left Minneapolis, we decided to purchase golf balls.

Now, I, being the artistic person I am, love colored golf balls. I'm not whacky about my colors, but I prefer something other than dull, old white balls. However at the store where we purchased them, in order to get the least expensive dozen we could, we had to buy a variety of colors: pink, gold, green and orange. We purchased them, believing we wouldn't have to use all of them. After all, how many balls can you lose in one game?

On the way to the golf course, Tom was mentioning to me that the club may match us up with another twosome. This was giving me a great deal of consternation because I had not played for about five years and even when I was playing regularly, I wasn't all that great. And this was no Par 3, this was a championship golf course!

When we arrived at the golf course, we discovered that yes, they had our reservations, but no, our clubs had not shown up. And in fact, the sales clerk had never even heard of such a thing: renting golf clubs and having them delivered to the golf course!!! "Most people", he informed us, "rent golf clubs from us." (We learned later when we got home that the golf clubs had shown up at an identically named golf course in Orlando!)

Tom then asked the price of renting golf clubs and the golf cart. It appeared that it would cost us about fifty-six dollars each for the rentals. Since we were there and all prepared to play, Tom decided to bite the bullet and pay the price. "Wait a minute," I said to the sales clerk, "Are you putting us with another twosome?" "Yes," he replied. "Well, in that case, why don't I just drive the cart and Tom, you can still play," I frantically suggested. I was more concerned with having to play with two expert strangers.

So we were assigned a threesome. The one couple never did introduce themselves, so we privately named them Ralph and Judy. But the other young man, Troy, shook hands with Tom and introduced himself.

Now, my husband really is a fair golfer. But on the first game of the season, until he gets into the rhythm of his swing, he hits all over the fairway. And as usual, he was hitting erratically. This didn't seem to bother Troy, the younger guy, but I came to the conclusion that Ralph was a perfectionist of the highest order and was either a former engineer or a military man, because it soon became obvious that he thought Tom would be better suited for a mini golf place.

On the second hole as Tom was teeing up, Ralph came up to him and kindly suggested that perhaps Tom would be happier if he continued on alone, that perhaps the "pressure" of playing with the other three wouldn't be so hard on him. Now, Tom, always believing the best in people, thought Ralph was just trying to be kind and assured him that he would really enjoy continuing with the three of them!

Ralph never said a thing to Tom for the rest of the game. Even when Tom parred a hole and none of the rest of them did, I don't think Ralph would have given Tom the time of day if he'd asked for it! Every time our golf cart got between Ralph and Judy and Troy's cart, Ralph would scoot around us and go chat with Troy about what other famous golf courses he had played. When the foursome parted ways, Troy again cordially shook hands with everyone around, but Ralph was probably muttering "good riddance" to Tom under his breath.

Oh, and remember those colorful balls we bought? Yes, they were there to haunt us too. Because this was an expert course, it had lots of water and lots of sand traps, and Tom kept losing balls in the water. The club actually gave us six white balls when we rented our clubs. But I thought, "Shoot, we've now got a dozen and a half balls, we'll never use up that many". But before I knew it, we were on to the colored balls.

I decided to dole them out, using the least innocuous color first and save the hot pinks until the very last. I have no idea what Ralph was thinking, but at every hole, it seemed like Tom was bringing out a new color ball! Fortunately we had not quite reached the pink balls before the end of the game.

You know, we really don't *try* to have adventures on our trips. They just seem to happen to us. But you wouldn't be the first of our friends to say: I'll never go on a trip with *you*!

WELL, JUST PRETEND...

There were a lot of "just pretends" on this camping trip – way too many for my taste.

You know, it's one thing when you plan on a camping trip that's non-electric and has no water hookup, it's another thing when you get there and discover there is none. And that's just what happened on our trip to Zippel Bay State Park on the shores of Lake of the Woods in Minnesota. Apparently, I didn't realize that "sixty drive-ups" meant just that.

My husband's mother grew up in nearby Warroad, MN, and we wanted to spend time in her old stomping grounds. Her father had a fishing career and even owned one of the islands in the middle of Lake of the Woods. AND, this would be a chance to see if we could camp for longer than just a weekend.

After all, I had finally gotten the camper set up inside so that it was a livable place and didn't look like a junk closet. I had bought drawers for our clothes, thus eliminating the need to bring along and stow the suitcase. And in the kitchen area, I eliminated the bins that we kept all our cutlery, dishes, cooking bowls, and paperware in by buying collapsible shelving. "A place for everything and everything in its place", as my dad used to say.

Zippel Bay was beautiful. Though my husband, Tom, and I were nearly out of gas when we got to the park, we drove up to the boat launch, six miles out of our way, and were duly impressed with the beauty of this area. After the drive back to the park ranger station, we found the campgrounds. We kept looking for the electrical sites and finally happened on some larger motor homes and stopped and asked where the electrical sites were, to which they replied, "there aren't any".

I have to admit that at this point in our camping experience, I had become accustomed to lights going on when I needed them, being able to plug in a fan on windless nights, running tap water right at my fingertips, and my thoughts were that we would just have to find another park in the area where these things were available. But my wise husband pointed out that it was already seven o'clock in the evening. He suggested that we camp here for tonight at least.

Due to that suggestion -it was just for overnight - we chose any old campsite and didn't even particularly look for the best place to park our camper - which was evident when we went to pull out my bed and had to move the camper due to the close proximity to a pine tree.

Tom assured me that we had a fully charged battery - he didn't tell me until the next day that he hadn't checked it to make sure of that truth since we had bought the camper two years earlier! And I must admit that I don't take much stock in my husband's mechanical abilities. So it was with great surprise and delight when the lights went on that first night. We wouldn't have to pretend we had electricity and running water after all.

Because it was dark by the time we got the camper set up, we didn't make a campfire that first night, but ate popcorn and cokes in the camper over a hot game of dominoes. Popcorn never tasted so good.

Our campsite was in the midst of pine and birch trees that rose four stories into the sky. It was difficult to even see the sky or the stars. But surprisingly, there were very few misquitoes out - perhaps the campground sprayed for them.

Earlier when we visited the bay, we noticed a sign posted on the bulletin board that announced that bears had been sighted in the three-thousand-acre park. Of course I didn't pay too much attention to the notice, but my husband, who had been here as a boy, remembered how his uncle had always carried a shotgun when they went blueberry picking, took the warning far more seriously. But of course he didn't tell me that.

With supper demolished and the game of dominoes over, it was soon time to go to bed. Have you ever noticed how dark and still it can be in the northern Minnesota woods? With little more than the stars four stories high for light, we turned in for the night, having closed up our sides and windows.

But in the middle of the night, I started feeling the need for some fresh air, so I began unzipping the canvas windows. Tom, awakening out of a sound sleep, thought it was bears scratching on the outside of the camper! Quickly, he was going through a rundown of potential weapons to ward the bear off, should he actually get into the camper. Could he use the new pancake griddle? Maybe he could stun him with it! What about the marshmallow forks? Maybe he could stab him! But finally, he realized I was merely unzipping the canvas sides. And so he could drift back to sleep with a sigh of relief.

The next morning we arose to sun filtering through the trees and supposedly a clear, sunny day. Due to the fact that we had survived the first night, we decided to stay after all and not pursue an electric site in another campground.

It turned out to be a great getaway. We hiked and swam in the bay, took a road trip into Warroad and discovered the electric campground was in the town, but it was packed and we couldn't have gotten in there without making a reservation a year ago anyway!

WHO STOLE THE SNOW

Home of sauerkraut, the Glockenspiel, Mozart, skiing in the Alps, Black Forest cake, Salzburg, the Autobahn, coffee so strong you could stand a spoon up in it and the home of my roots: Germany. It was a longtime dream of mine to travel to the birthplace of my ancestors.

Having had two years of German in high school, I was sure I would be fluent amongst the natives in no time. My husband, Tom tried to warn me that my high school German classes had been a long, long time ago – about 40 years to be exact, and that it may not come back to me that easily. "Nonsense," I cried, I'm sure it will be a snap! Of course what I hadn't taken into consideration is that learning to speak German in a class and speaking conversational German were two entirely different things.

We decided to go to Germany in the winter for two reasons. One, I was a very poor flier. Air pockets made me nervous. So Tom reasoned that flying in the wintertime in cooler air would greatly reduce the likelihood of air turbulence. Secondly, we loved to cross country ski, so why not ski the Alps?

The trip's inception actually happened in Louisville, Kentucky where we were living. We were doing better financially because Tom had a great job there and we were completely out of debt. So we began to plan our dream vacation. The only problem was that towards the end of the year, Tom lost his job and we were forced to move to Indianapolis, Indiana three hours north of Louisville. But since we had already booked our flight out of Louisville, we had no choice but to travel back to Louisville three days after moving in to our Indianapolis house!

It was a whirlwind move. I was throwing things in cupboards as fast as the movers were bringing in the boxes. My husband, who had already begun his new job there, complained that every day his breakfast cereal was located in a different cupboard. I kept moving things around because I didn't have time to think through where I wanted to put everything, and yet my time was limited before we would be taking off for Europe.

We also had a new puppy, a six-week-old black lab named Joyful 3 whom we had purchased while in Louisville. And we also had a boarder, a man who was also starting at the same company as my husband, who needed a place to stay until his new home was ready to move into, Bill Barker. Bill would be puppy and house sitting while we were in Europe for ten days.

The night before we were leaving, Bill helped me pack the skis. I had searched with no success for a ski container to take on the plane, but all they had was cases for downhill skis. So Bill helped me devise a covering for the skis: a couple of sleeping bags and duct tape!

We were down to the wire upon heading out to Louisville and I couldn't for the life of me find my snow boots. But this was so typical of me and packing boxes. I had such good intentions to pack only the same kinds of things in one box, but then I'd find extra space left over in a box and end up putting any old thing I could cram into that space. So my boots weren't in with the rest of our clothing and shoes. (When we got home, I found them in the box with the shovels)!

So when we reached Louisville, I had to stop and buy boots at Sarnoff's in Middletown. Unfortunately, they didn't have my size, so I had to get a couple of sizes bigger. Also, since I knew it would be constant snow in Germany, I didn't bring any regular shoes. Just planned to walk around everywhere in my boots.

When we arrived in Munich after our long flight, we found it to be downright balmy out! No snow! Apparently, it was an off year in the Alps for snow where in previous years they had as much as five feet of snow everywhere. So I clunked around Europe in my extra large boots on dry pavement for the entire ten days we were there.

Being too cheap to take the train, we decided to rent a car for the trip. Naturally my husband chose an economy car because gas in Europe is much higher than in the states. We were also trusting in his good memory, from a couple trips he took here in his college days, to remember how to get places. The only problem was fitting the long cross-country skis into an economy car. The only way they fit was over the seats crosswise either hitting the driver in the head or the passenger. My husband decided to bite the bullet and let them hit his head.

He also wanted a stick shift because it got better gas mileage. That was fine with me because we had planned for him to do all the driving considering the high speeds traveled on the Autobahn and the winding roads. That only backfired on us once. Upon leaving the resort in Bad Ausie, Vienna, Tom got an excruciatingly bad headache from all the strong caffeine in their coffee, and for about a couple of hours, it looked like I might be relearning how to drive a stick shift – but in the Alps! However, the resort owners were nice enough to allow us to stay past checkout time so that Tom's headache could abate.

Our first stop was Berchtesgaden where Tom, in his college days, visited the Eagles Nest, a weekend retreat for Hitler. Though we had reservations, they had not turned on the heat in our room. It was radiator heated, extremely slow to heat up and we were cold most of our stay there. We ended up sleeping with all our clothes on between the two featherbed mattresses. It's a wonder we didn't smother!

Another rude awakening in the hotel is that they offered towels, but no washcloths. So we had to dampen the end of our towel and use it both to wash and dry ourselves.

Our first evening meal in Germany, I insisted on using a German menu – just sure that my German would come back quickly and I'd be able to figure out what we were eating. Thankfully, another German couple who spoke English helped me to peruse the menu.

This was the beginning of my love for Schnitzel. Every night I was in Germany, I ordered a different kind – or maybe that was the only thing I could read on the menu. On a trip to Munich, Tom and I discovered the Schnitzel Palace where we ordered a Schnitzel platter that contained various kinds of Schnitzel and vegetables and just about covered the entire table. At one point we looked up and noticed the chef and wait staff peeking out at these two Americans eating their fare. That was the biggest meal we had there.

Meals in Germany and perhaps throughout Europe aren't like meals in the U.S. The portions are smaller, but adequate. Salads are not automatically served with the meals, but are available. And no refills on Coca-Cola. In fact, though they were always served cold, it was a privilege if you got ice in your coke. You learned how to make your beverage last throughout the meal.

Breakfast was generally what is considered continental: cold cuts, cheese, hard rolls, only one butter per person and jams and coffee. You never got a hot meal. But we learned to enjoy less and be satisfied.

From Berchtesgaden, we traveled to Bad Ausie where our week's reserved timeshare was located. While the accommodations were nice, nothing was extravagant in them.

The German people had learned how to make do with less. For instance, we made a trip to the grocery store after unpacking and the hausfraus, as the housewives were called, traveled to the supermarket on bicycles carrying their own shopping bags in the form of a basket. Thus, they only purchased what they needed immediately. You paid extra for the grocery store to provide bags.

While at the resort, due to the fact that there was no snow, we decided to travel on day trips. One day we went to Schubert's home city. Another day we went back to Munich with the hopes of seeing the Glockenspiel, a larger than life sized clock in the downtown area. Known the world over, and we couldn't figure out how to get there.

This was one of the downsides of taking a car. Where we Americans think it means more freedom and less control by others, the train would have taken us right into the center of Munich where we could have easily seen the Glockenspiel. But we circled the city several times, trying to take this exit or that exit and to no avail. Since we were flying out of Munich at the end of our trip, we finally gave up and decided to come back the last day to see the Glockenspiel.

The town of Bad Ausie was typical of old style German towns. The street was so narrow in places that only one car could pass through at a time. So we drove into it sparingly, afraid we would get in an accident. We went to town mostly for dinner.

One night they had some kind of Laborer's Festival harolding the working class jobs. People dressed up like maids and shoemakers and butlers and then acted out their role in the restaurants and bar. One young woman approached Tom and asked if she could shine his shoes. He let her pretend to shine his suede shoes.

All of the restaurants were a combination bar and grill because everybody drinks beer with their meals. But their pubs felt different than American bars. They were just a part of the restaurant, not a place to tell your troubles to the bartender or pick up a date for the evening.

Another interesting facet about German restaurants is that people brought their dogs in them. The dogs were usually big and old and just laid on the floor next to their master until he finished his meal. Having a dog myself, I wished America would incorporate that rule. But then I could picture some yippy little thing barking at all the new customers coming in the restaurant.

There was a beautiful mountain stream close to our resort where we took a walk one Sunday afternoon. It took us about an hour and a half to get to the end of the line and then of course we had to walk back. On the way back I was getting desperate to find a bathroom, so we stopped at a hotel across the stream. I decided to try out my German on them. So I said, "Wo ist die Badenzimmer?" (literally: "Where is the bathroom?" And the woman replied to me in English, "Oh, you vant a room with a bath?" So I replied to her in English and said, "No, I need to use a bathroom." She just shook her head at me and said, "Vee haf no public toileten". So I danced all the way back to the resort praying I wouldn't have an accident.

After Bad Ausie we traveled to downtown Vienna. Unfortunately we got to our hotel during rush hour traffic. Having gotten to the train station, we were able to make reservations via phone. Then pre-GPS days, we attempted to find our way to the hotel. We kept circling the blocks like a dog sniffing out a bone, each time making our circles smaller and smaller until we finally honed in on the hotel. It was one of the few places that had a parking lot for the guests.

Our original plan was to travel by train into Prague, my husband's roots, because we heard that bandits stripped the rental cars of their tires. But then we learned that though Prague was only a couple of hours away by car, it would take the train eight hours because it was a milk run train, stopping at every little town along the route. So we scratched that idea and traveled on instead to other parts of Germany.

It was our pure delight to stay mostly in Bed and Breakfasts. Because of the time of year, there were many open for business. We eagerly toodled up to the door of any B and B that said, "Zimmer Frei", which means we have a vacancy. In some place, English was spoken fluently and in others we barely made ourselves understood between my sketchy high school German and their sketchy English. I found that in conversing with them, they would say a word in German and about ten seconds later, I would get it and make some type of attempt to answer my host while he continued to rattle on. It made for very stilted conversations.

Mostly we toured southern Germany. One day, while traveling, we came across the equivalent of the American speed trap. There was a narrowing from a four-lane road to a two-lane road and a policeman who had hollowed out his police van and put a desk in it in which to catch unsuspecting motorists.

Tom assumed all the people pulled to the side of the road surely must not have anything to do with him, and in an attempt to get around a truck in front of him so he wouldn't be stuck behind him on the two-lane, made a beeline to get around him before the road narrowed. The policeman saw it as an attempt to avoid the speed trap and ran out in the middle of the road, waving his arms and crying "Halt! Halt!"

So like all of the other motorists before us, we joined the throng awaiting arrest. I had visions of spending an overnight in the local German jail for fleeing the police.

The policeman did not speak English, it soon became apparent, as he ushered Tom unceremoniously out of the car with a series of hand signals. While Tom was taking out our passports, the policeman gestured to the sleeping-bagged, duct-taped pair of skis resting across the seat. I was afraid it looked like a beluga gun and he would think we were carrying dangerous weapons. Tom must have made him understand that they were skis – at least we did not have to remove them from the car to prove it.

Also, using the universal language for money by rubbing his thumb and first finger together, the policeman quickly made it understood that in order to get out of this mess, Tom needed to pay up. He ushered him back to his mobile office, having helped himself to whatever it cost from Tom's wallet. And having escaped imprisonment, we were soon on our way.

Two days before we were due to fly back home, we drove to Munich, determined to once again see the famed Gloockenspiel. But when we arrived at our bed and breakfast that evening, which was an inn over a bar, I had contracted some type of flu bug and lay dying most of the night in between hourly trips to the bathroom. At one point from my perch in the bathroom, I looked out at Tom lying face down on the bed, probably wishing he could die too, overcome by the fumes emanating from me.

And once again, we didn't get to the Glockenspiel that day or the next. It would have to wait for another trip.

WILL THIS NIGHT NEVER END???

I don't know why it is, but Tom, my husband loved the idea of fall camping. He cherished the idea of sleeping in a cold tent with just your nose sticking out seeing your breath and not even wanting to roll over in your sleeping bag and leave the warm spot you've created. He loved sitting around the campfire in the fifty-degree evening, shivering. He claimed it was because his mother used to bundle him up as a baby and leave him out on their screen porch in the fall and winter days of Minnesota. On the other hand, I wanted nothing to do with sitting and sleeping in the cold.

So, as he did just about every year, he wanted to go fall camping. At my aghast look, he assured me he would keep me warm. "We can cuddle," he declared. "Yeah, right," I thought, "that may take care of the time in the sleeping bag, but what about all the other times out in the cold, like mealtimes and sitting around the campfire?" "It will be fun," he assured me.

Mind you, I loved camping too, but let's be reasonable. Camping is for summertime, not the fall. But as usual I grudgingly went along with his plan. Our destination this year was Hoosier Horse Park down in southern Indiana. I was hoping "southern" meant warmer, but alas, it did not. However, this trip cured my husband's desire for camping in the cold once and for all!

It was one of those Indian summer days that we set off on, packed to the gills with camping equipment and the dog. You know, those fall sunny days when it can get up to eighty during the day, the air smells like smoke and the vibrant colors of the trees against a blue cloudless sky.

I guess we must have downplayed the "horse" part of this plan. All around us you could hear horses snorting as they waited to be taken out riding by their masters on the wooded trails.

It always amazed me that it seemed that one of the purposes in camping was to get us out of our house mentality to enjoy nature, but one of the first things I did upon arrival was to designate the "rooms" of my camping spot.

There was the living room where the campfire would be with foldup chairs surrounding it and a lantern nearby for a light at night. There was the kitchen, which usually consisted of a heavy, weathered picnic table upon which I set up my stove and cooler. And then there was the bedroom, the actual tent itself. So much for getting away from the idea of a house!

In the late afternoon on our first day after setting up our living quarters, we went hiking in the beautiful woods in that area and discovered that there were even backpackers who left their cars in the parking lot and hiked in to their camping spots. They must have been carrying far less equipment than we packed.

We had reserved two glorious nights in this wonder spot - or at least that was my husband's thinking. My thinking was more like: two grueling nights to endure the cold.

Though tenters, we at least slept on camping cots so that we weren't directly on the ground. But our sleeping bags were cheap ones we had brought into our marriage and probably didn't go down much below seventy degrees. Though Tom piled several blankets on top of me to make sure I stayed warm (I'm sure he did this to ensure many more fall camping trips to come), it was never the snug as a bug in a rug comfort in which he hoped I would be.

With our dog curled up between us on a blanket on the floor, we drifted off to sleep to the sounds of snorting horses. For me, it was a fitful sleep at best. It seemed I would sleep for a short time and then check my watch to see how many hours I had left until daylight. At two a.m., I again checked my watch and thought, "Will this night never end?" To my dismay, we had at least another five hours of dark before the daylight and then another cold day before the cold night.

But lo and behold, it seemed that Tom was having the same issues with cold and sleeplessness that I was having. In one of my many watch checking moments, he finally spoke and said, "Can't you sleep either?"

Once we deduced that we were both sleepless and freezing, we decided to pack up our temporary house and head home. Unlike the neat packing for the trip there, we literally threw our rolled up tent and belongings in the station wagon.

Throughout the entire hour and a half drive home, my husband had the heat on high. Even when we got back home, we couldn't warm up and both of us decided to take hot baths before we jumped into our nice, warm, electrically heated beds.

Yes, sir, that is the camping trip that broke Tom's yearly declaration that he *loved* fall camping trips. In years to come, if he even began to hint at fall camping, I had only to remind him of Hoosier Horse Park and the idea died on his lips.

ARE YOU SURE ABOUT THIS???

The whole move seemed to hinge on the estate sale lady! And she really was just supposed to be a minor part of this story! Every time we tried to get in earlier or change direction, she rose up like a formidable obstacle blocking our every move. It seemed that she ruled with an iron fist and when she said "jump", everybody said "how high?" But let me back up.

It was in February of 2009 that Tom, my husband lost his job. He had been contracting for an insurance company for the past year and a half, but they were laying off people due to a lack of funds and a downturn in the economy. We felt the Lord telling us to get our house ready. So naturally I assumed we would be moving in conjunction with his job. But as it turned out, he got another contracting job six months later and we really wouldn't have had to move after all. However, since we were poised to move and since it was so terribly expensive living where we did in Fargo, we decided to put our house on the market and move to San Antonio, Texas.

Then began eight months of waiting for the house to sell. We heard every reason in the book as to why it wasn't selling. If it wasn't the economy, it was because our house wasn't the "much cherished" open floor plan every buyer wanted or because we didn't have a triple car garage or because our basement wasn't totally finished or because we didn't have a master bath and closet. Our hopes went up and down with each prospective buyer that toured our house.

Then one Saturday we had a call that not one, but two people were interested in purchasing our home. It seemed too good to be true after all these months of nothing. A new family toured it in the morning and a return buyer toured it in the afternoon. It was the latter, however, who made a bid to purchase our six-year-old home that we had built.

Perhaps it was the realtor's lingo or something else, but we understood the offer was for three thousand dollars more than our asking price, but they, in turn, were asking that we pay all the taxes for the forthcoming year (about six thousand dollars) and they wanted to take possession in three weeks. While we thought that was a bit steep, we agreed to it. It wasn't until we got to Texas that we discovered we actually paid fourteen thousand dollars extra! It must have been something our realtor forgot to tell us.

The buyers were excited about their new house. On the day of inspection, everything went off without a hitch until I opened my big mouth and told them about the fountain pump that had gone out in the back yard. I told them where they could get a new one, thinking I was being helpful, but their realtor was a barracuda in women's clothing and negotiated for us to purchase a new one for them as well. Me and my big mouth.

About that time the neighbor behind us informed us that we were two feet over his lot line and that he wanted to put up a privacy fence. That made the buyers really nervous.

As we explained to our neighbor, we hadn't set out to defraud anyone, but we were the first people to build a house on Norman Court and the semi professionals who put the fence in thought they were on the lot line when, in fact, they were over.

But we found a fence company that our neighbor was satisfied with and who offered to take my fence down for free. Though the buyers loved the picket fence, they would lose it in the back.

But now, having this fear of being over on the back lot line, they wanted the sides checked as well. Though the neighbor building his home next to us was not demanding that we take our fence down, which also happened to be two feet over on the lot line, the buyers in their anguish, decided we should pay for the moving of that fence as well. With all the extras they were asking for and I was offering out of the goodness of my heart, I began to wonder if they wanted us to support them for the first year as well!

The money the buyers were using was a death benefit. Sadly, they lost their oldest son in the Iraq war, but he had an insurance policy and had designed it so that they could purchase a home with it. That's where we came in.

Due to the quick amount of time they wanted to take possession of the home, that made it a real crunch time for us to get to San Antonio and purchase home and get back to Fargo to pack.

But God was with us. We found a home within a couple of days in San Antonio. So attempting to save on the motel bill, car rental and the amount of time Tom was losing from work, we quickly got our "nonrefundable" airline tickets changed to get back to Fargo in record time.

However, two days before the move out date, the buyers informed us that they had not yet gotten the death benefit check from the government. The military tried to tell them that they had neglected to fill out one form and thus, it would be another six weeks! Thankfully, the buyers had proof that they had indeed filled out this form and faxed them a copy of it. So the military said they would expedite it.

We couldn't really change our plans because we also had set too many things in motion. The moving company was set to arrive the next day and we had plans to stay overnight with some friends on the second night of our trip to Texas. So we took off for our cross- country excursion. Tom drove the Volvo wagon pulling the camper and I followed in the van we had inherited from my mom.

We really thought we were well prepared for the trip. We had purchased two cell phones so that we could communicate with each other. Not having had cell phones before, we were novices in using them and the first day of the trip I got some strange 1-800 number calling me that I couldn't answer, ignore nor turn it off. It kept me from calling out and eventually totally drained my battery. The only way I could communicate with Tom in his car was to send up smoke signals or race around him, gesturing wildly to get him to pull over at the next exit or rest stop.

We only had one mishap that second day out. We lost the battery on the camper in stages. And because my cell phone was now defunct, there was no way for me to communicate to Tom. So I just watched helplessly as I saw the different parts careening down the highway. In southern Kansas I saw the top of the battery go. Then in northern Oklahoma I saw the bottom of the battery case go and closer to Oklahoma City, I finally saw the rest of the battery skidding onto the shoulder.

That second evening, we were due to arrive in Oklahoma City and stay with friends. We thought we had plenty of time to drive that day – we figured it was only about six hours, so Tom decided to slow down to sixty due to the pull on the engine of his Volvo wagon with the camper. But because of his slower speed, it ended up taking us closer to eight hours to get to our friends' home. Thinking we were arriving earlier in the day, they had planned to show us around the city and get some good visiting in.

It also seemed that they had invited everyone in their family over that evening for supper. I didn't know we were such honored guests. They had invited their daughter and her family, friends of their daughter's, her aunt and several other people. And here we were, arriving late. But in true southern style, they accepted us whenever we arrived.

The next day we were on the last leg of our trip – only eight hours to go if Tom kept the speed up. From southern Oklahoma City down to San Antonio, the traffic was much heavier. It had also begun to rain, which further dampened our spirits. We were doing fine until we got to Fort Worth, Texas. That's when the unthinkable happened. I say "unthinkable" because we never even thought it *could* happen. We had no Plan B. Our cell phones were originally Plan B, but that was, of course, out of the question now.

I must admit that I thought the worst thing that could happen was if I got pulled over by the police for some reason and Tom continued traveling happily down the freeway. Without any phone and only a sketchy idea of how to get to our final destination, that fear worried me.

But that isn't what happened in Fort Worth. Tom got into what I knew was an exit off of the freeway an onto another freeway. There was so much traffic and it wasn't easy maneuvering the car and the camper from lane to lane. I was behind him at that point and was able to move over. I slowed a bit, hoping that he would see and move back into my lane, but he didn't. So I had no alternative in that heavy traffic, but to keep traveling south.

The Lord said two things to me: "Don't panic" and "Don't get off the freeway, just slow your speed down and keep heading south." I figured if Tom had to turn around and I was going slow enough that he would eventually pass me again.

I kept looking in my rearview mirror, and lo and behold, about twenty minutes later, here comes Tom's Volvo. I rolled down my window and waved, but when he went by me, he didn't even look at me. And I thought, oh, boy, how am I going to let him know we're back together again?

So every time we passed someone, I'd dangle my van out in the passing lane a little longer, so Tom would be sure to see me. It wasn't until we stopped for gas a little later that Tom told me he never even knew I was not behind him!

In San Antonio, we had rented a short-term living place for three weeks. The pictures of the place online were greatly exaggerated. They showed a bed, a love seat and living room area and a kitchenette complete with dishes, cookware, silverware and a refrigerator and stove. Believing we had a living room space, I brought a foldable table and planned to use the kitchen chairs to sit on and do our work.

What a rude awakening for us. There was no living room or couch. It had one easy chair in it and the kitchen chairs were stools that would have put us up higher than the table. So we had to set up our workspace on the kitchen counter connected to the wall, which meant that if we used it to eat off of, we had to move our keyboards and peek at each other through Tom's two monitors while we ate. It cut down on our conversation considerably. And passing food back and forth under or around the monitors was quite a challenge as well. All you saw was the hand of the other person at the table.

We later learned that there were other larger Studio 6 apartments available, but the manager put us in the smallest one and just didn't bother to tell us about any other options. And being the fine upstanding Christians we were, we didn't want to complain, so we just tried to work with situation.

What could it hurt? We were only going to be there for three weeks! NOT. When we went to sign the title with the title company, because my husband forgot to wire the money to pay for the house from his T. Rowe Price account and neither the official presiding over the signing of the title nor the homeowner from whom we were purchasing the house trusted us, the house wouldn't be ours until the money arrived. So we had to stay in our dinky apartment for another week. That night after we got that news, I broke down and cried for all of the disappointments we were facing.

The homeowner did, however, allow the moving van to store our furniture in the garage of the house we were purchasing. The following day we went over to the house and I seriously considered pulling out the hide-a-bed from our sofa and sleeping in the garage until our money was wired.

But finally, we got our money, signed the title and moved in to our new house. And of course we lived happily ever after.

ARE YOU FLEXIBLE YET?

We loved Florida. Having honeymooned in the St. Petersburg Beach area, we came back about every other year. On one trip, we decided to have a goal. Realizing how much we tend to grumble on trips when things didn't go the way we wanted them to, this one year we decided to work on being more flexible.

Due to being cheap, instead of flying into Tampa, we flew to Orlando, home of Disney World and Mickey Mouse. We saved a lot of money flying into this area, but we well made up for it in gas money and time driving down to St. Petersburg.

Heading south on the freeway, we decided to stop off in a few little towns along the way. The first sign that drew us was an announcement of a strawberry festival on a billboard. Now, I not only loved to eat strawberries, but my kitchen was decorated in them. It started out when I bought strawberry wallpaper one year and people began giving me strawberry decorations for my kitchen. Before I knew it, I was locked into a strawberry decor. But I didn't care, I loved red and the look of strawberries, so I just stayed in that mode in every kitchen I owned.

The billboard announced that this town was the Strawberry Capitol of the World! It also spoke glowingly of the annual Strawberry Festival. Of course I had to go check it out for myself. We stopped in a restaurant for a bite to eat and learned that the Strawberry Festival was actually last week. But the waitresses in this restaurant were still sporting strawberry T-shirts. I just had to have one, so we asked one of the waitresses where we could find some.

Since the festival was over, she sent us driving out in the country somewhere to find a trailer where they were keeping the overflow T-shirts. We found the T-shirts okay and each bought one. But on the way back, we got stuck in the sand. I guess we had an especially low rental car.

As we were pushing the car, I asked my husband, "Are you flexible yet?" To which he replied, "I'm flexible." The problem was that the car wasn't flexible and we soon learned that we needed help getting out of the sand. We walked down a road that sported some houses on it, but every place we stopped it seemed that nobody was home. So we eventually made our way back to our car to wait for someone to come along (this was precell phones).

Eventually someone did show up and agreed for a price to tow our car out. We sat in the back of his pickup truck gazing at our car as the man drove us back to a main road so we could continue on our way. But at least I had my strawberry T-shirt!

THE RETRO TRIP

"I think we've already been on this block before", I mumbled in dismay. Little did I know how often I would be repeating that same phrase in the two hours we were in Dallas.

We took a trip up to the Texas State Fair this weekend - got to know Dallas quite well because we kept going around and around on the same blocks. We Googled where our motel was, but Google didn't take into consideration that during State Fair time, there were streets blocked off because the State Fair has about fifteen thousand gates to it.

We asked lots of people for directions. We finally called the motel, and some Indian guy was trying to talk me in. After I hung up without victory, we decided to let our dog out, and while tending to her, we spotted a policeman and asked for directions. He asked where we were staying and upon hearing the name, he said, "you don't want to stay there." And I said, "but we've got reservations and they'll take our dog too." And he said "lady, that hotel is known for bad goings on here in Dallas (he didn't elaborate, but I got the impression it was either drugs or prostitution). He told me the police frequented that hotel quite a bit.

When he heard we were from San Antonio, he informed me that he had once been a policeman in San Antonio, and Dallas wasn't like nice, quiet little San Antonio. He suggested we get back on I-35 South and get some motel outside of Dallas that would be safe.

So after wandering around Dallas for two hours, we finally, at ten o'clock that night, said we have no choice but to return to San Antonio. We don't know this city and we don't have a laptop to go try to find other reservations, so we might as well just go home.

Out of the city limits, however we found a Red Roof that takes dogs (we called it the Wed Woof), and we stayed overnight there and went to the State Fair the next day. Unfortunately, we paid twenty dollars for parking (five dollars more than the legitimate State Fair lots would have been!).

Aside from the fact that it is very, very expensive to attend the TX State Fair (everything is bought with coupons and anything really good was ten or more coupons, the equivalent of five dollars). Tom actually got me to go on the ferris wheel - I never go on rides, but I watched it long enough to discover it didn't plunge to the ground leaving my stomach up in the air before it takes the plunge. We figured with the price of tickets and all, we spent around two hundred fifty dollars.

IN THE BEGINNING...

Our love for traveling came from the families we grew up in: Middle-class families, each with two kids, and both grew up in the 1950s.

Back then, airplane travel was just for the traveling man. Our trips usually took place in cars with no air conditioning, wide-open windows, while fighting for space with our older brothers. In my case, it also included a big hairy English Springer Spaniel in a four-seater Oldsmobile sedan. Talk about crowded!

Although my father traveled for a living, he still looked forward to his four weeks of vacation, two spent up at Elbow Lake in northern Minnesota in the summer and two weeks during the winter to a warmer climate like Arizona or California, and even once to Florida.

Tom and I were both in our twenties when we met. He was twenty-nine and I was twenty-three. We met at a single adults' group that was part of a large Lutheran Church in downtown Minneapolis. We actually formally met in the Monday night Bible study. The truth is in joining, we were both looking for a mate, but found the Lord first and then each other.

Tom, at the time I met him, was engaged to a young woman, but it was more of a one-sided love affair. He was so eager to be a married man that he proposed to the first pretty girl he found. But Bonnie wasn't the one God had chosen for him. I was.

After dating a few months, Tom proposed to me at a retreat in northern Minnesota. I remember it well. We were out walking on some trail and found a grassy knoll. Tom began to say the words and I said, "I want a proposal on your knees." His classic response was: One knee for you and two for the Lord."

During our engagement year, Tom lived in our future marital residence in St. Louis Park and I lived up in Brooklyn Center with my parents. After work every day, I drove over to his house and stayed with him for the evening, then drove back home to my parents' house.

It was a good thing we were engaged for a whole year because ours was a rocky relationship, mostly, because of me - I had major anger issues. Most nights when I left to go home, you could hear me screeching the tires on my 1970 Pontiac due to something which I was mad at Tom for.

As tumultuous as our relationship was, Tom never gave up on me. I asked him multiple times why he wanted to marry me (I knew how difficult I was), and he said the Lord enabled him to see my heart, that I was angry only on the outside, but that I had a godly heart. Though I was quick to get angry, I also was willing to say "I'm sorry, I was wrong." And Tom, ever the peacemaker, readily forgave me.

So on October 26, 1974 (a date Tom said God had given him) we got married in the Lutheran church where we met. Tom had a Toyota with a stick shift, which I did not know how to drive. So before our wedding, my father took me out in his car and taught me how to drive. My biggest fear was coordinating the clutch and accelerator. I was so afraid of stalling that I kept my foot on the clutch too long. Thus we zipped around corners at an alarming rate of speed.

In teaching me how to go in reverse, we went to an empty parking lot where Dad set up scenarios for me. He said, "Let's say you're parked at a curb and the guy ahead of you has car trouble, what are you going to do? And I said, "I'm going to wait right here until the tow truck comes to take his car away, so I can drive forward." Such were my teachings.

On our honeymoon, Tom let me do my driving stints mostly on the freeways and he drove through the towns. But I remember one time when we were about to cross a railroad track and it was on a little hill. All of a sudden, I panicked and asked if he would drive. He was in the passenger's side in his stocking feet, but he dutifully got out of the car and ran around to the driver's side in front of the long line of traffic behind us so he could drive over the hill.

We honeymooned in St. Petersburg, Florida. But I am sorry to say due to my anger issues, we fought more than anything in those first two weeks.

By the time we returned home, Tom had a traveling sales job lined up in the state of Washington as a book salesman through Bethany Fellowship. His territory was Montana, Idaho, Oregon, Washington and northern California.

His Toyota Celica was packed to the hilt. We had one suitcase between the two of us (I was a frugal packer), an electric frying pan my mother insisted we take in case we got tired of eating in restaurants, my guitar in the back seat, and his four book bags in the trunk.

The scenery was magnificent in the Pacific northwest. Lush green grass, cold crisp air in the mountains, inviting rivers everywhere. We kept our bathing suits handy and if it got too hot on our travels, we changed clothes in the car and plunged into a refreshing river. With Tom's expense account, we could stay in inexpensive motels and dine like kings.

We sampled Dungeness crab, a sweet roll called a Butterhorn, steak, pancake houses (new to the Pacific Northwest in the '70s) BBQ at Love's BBQ pit and great crab sandwiches at the Crabbage Patch. And then on Sunday after church, because by that time we were longing for home cooked food, we made our way to a restaurant called "The Turkey House" in Everett, Washington near where we lived in the Motel 6, where you had to pay 50 cents extra for a TV in your room!

Sunday evenings we went to a local park to have hamburgers on the grill. We didn't have a spatula, so we fashioned a long, flat piece of wood into one and used that to flip the hamburgers.

But Tom was exceedingly homesick, more so than me. Every time we passed a sign on the freeway heading west, he would pretend the car was turning there automatically. He would wrestle with the steering wheel to make it look like the car wanted to go back to MN. So just about every weekend, you would find us on our knees by the bed, praying that God would help us endure our current calling. I think for me what kept me going was a desire to save face. I didn't want to have to go home and admit to my parents we failed and hear them gloat, "I told you so."

Besides staying at the Motel 6, the pastor of the church we were attending offered us a small trailer near his house. The first night we used it, we got there very late. The pastor had given us a key before, so we didn't need to disturb him.

We got in the camper and it was cold in the spring in Everett. We didn't know how to turn on the heater, so Tom said, "I'm going to teach you an old Army trick: Sleeping between two mattresses. The only problem was that these mattresses didn't mold to your body because they were foam rubber. So the corners bounced up. We just slept close to each other with one mattress over us.

The pastor was mortified in the morning to learn that we had slept in that cold camper, and quickly showed us how to turn on the heater (on which I later dropped Tom's pajama tops which gave them a waffle pattern on the back). It had no indoor toilet, so the pastor said we could go in the house whenever we needed to. But I was a newlywed and too embarrassed to admit I had to go to the bathroom, so I went to the bathroom out in the woods. The only problem was the woods were full of slugs, which were like small slimy snails. I heard that if you poured salt on them, they would shrivel up and die. So I carried a Morton salt container with me every time I went out there, sprinkling salt as I went.

The church we attended in Everett was a small nondenominational one. But it was the people there who taught me about hospitality. Many times we would get in too late, for the motel and we would showed up at someone's house and they pulled their kids out of bed to make room for us.

They became like family to us. And by the time we left to go back to MN, we had made forever friends. It was the pastor who encouraged us to go back home to MN. He said, "If anything could break up your marriage, the strain of your current living condition would do it. But I can see that you are on solid ground."

As of this writing, we have been married 50 years. We still enjoy traveling. Tom finally went into underwriting for life insurance companies as his career. We moved five times during out marriage having to do with his job, and each time it afforded us the opportunity to find new places in which to live and travel.